LINCOLN CHRISTIA

W9-CCW-246

# THE CHURCH
# IN THE EDUCATION
# OF THE PUBLIC

# THE CHURCH IN THE EDUCATION OF THE PUBLIC

REFOCUSING THE
TASK OF RELIGIOUS
EDUCATION

## JACK L. SEYMOUR
## ROBERT T. O'GORMAN
## CHARLES R. FOSTER

•

Abingdon Press
Nashville

THE CHURCH IN THE EDUCATION OF THE PUBLIC:
REFOCUSING THE TASK OF RELIGIOUS EDUCATION

*Copyright © 1984 by Abingdon Press*

All rights reserved.
No part of this book may be reproduced in any manner
whatsoever without written permission of the publisher
except brief quotations embodied in critical articles
or reviews. For information address Abingdon Press,
Nashville, Tennessee.

**Library of Congress Cataloging in Publication Data**

SEYMOUR, JACK L. (JACK LEE), 1948–
   The church in the education of the public.
   1. Christian education—United States.
   2. Church and education—United States.
   I. O'Gorman, Robert T. (Robert Thomas), 1941–  .
   II. Foster, Charles R., 1937–  . III. Title.
   BV1467.S39      1984      377'.8'0973     84-6203

**ISBN 0-687-08252-8**

MANUFACTURED BY THE PARTHENON PRESS AT
NASHVILLE, TENNESSEE, UNITED STATES OF AMERICA

*To*
*Donald Welch,*
*President of Scarritt College*

77127

# CONTENTS

# F O R E W O R D

In 1981, Scarritt College in Nashville, Tennessee, called together a new faculty. We who responded to that call had been enticed away from our previous positions by the vision of new graduate programs in Christian education and church music to be developed in cooperation with Vanderbilt Divinity School. With our colleagues Millie Goodson and Leo Rippy, we were immediately confronted by the necessity for developing a course of study for the new program. To facilitate our conversations, the three of us agreed to cooperate in organizing and teaching the foundations course of the curriculum. We felt this experience would help focus our expectations and clarify our individual assumptions regarding a course of study that might both reflect and shape the field and the discipline.

The experiment proved useful at both these points. Even more, it provided the impetus for this book. When we accepted our positions on the faculty, each knew of the others' interest in the history of religious education. What we did not know was that our historical inquiries tended to concentrate upon the relationship between churches' educational efforts and the educational issues and concerns of the larger community. The public, especially that public which makes up

9

the United States, was the concern of our research; the role of church education in shaping the public mind and ethos, the subject of our inquiry. As Chuck Foster began to tell the story of nineteenth-century Protestant commitments and strategies, Jack Seymour did the same for progressive Protestant religious educators, and Bob O'Gorman paralleled both eras with Catholic perspectives on the church's educational mission, we discerned continuities we previously had not seen and differences we had overlooked. We discovered one, rather than two stories. Indeed, as we envision it, the interplay of Catholic and Protestant education in the United States until Vatican II might be illustrated by the movements of two dancers on a common stage, seemingly caught up in the privacy of their own interpretations. Closer observation, however, reveals the interdependence of movement, linked not only by the common space of the stage but by the rhythms and themes of the musical score.

It is that story we have chosen to tell together. In our first chapter we establish the framework for our discussion of the interdependence of Christian churches and the public in national life, and the necessary role of church education in helping to shape public consciousness. In the second chapter we begin to trace the reasons for the abdication of Protestant church education from its public role. In the process we explore nineteenth-century Protestant views of the public and the tension between those views and the educational strategies increasingly advocated by church leaders. The third chapter turns to the simultaneous quest by Catholics for an education that is responsive to both the authority of the church in the common life and the democratic ideals of the nation. The early twentieth-century attempts of progressive Protestant religious educators to reclaim the church's role in the formation of the public constitutes the focus of our fourth chapter.

In our study we have become increasingly aware of the

tendency in the church, both Protestant and Catholic, to lose sight of its public role, to concentrate its energies upon educating people into church life and ecclesiastical responsibilities. This domestication of the church's educational efforts has increasingly dominated the educational commitments of church leaders since the great depression, and especially after World War II. Consequently in our final chapter, we again raise the question that prompted the concern of so many early church leaders: What is the role of church education in shaping national values, ideology, and life-style? It is a question we believe has been ignored much too long.

In the following reflections, we are aware of the significant contributions made by other religious faiths, particularly Judaism, in forming the United States public life. We believe that any contemporary understanding must recognize the presence and contribution of religious pluralism. The creation of a homogeneous public would recognize neither the depth of religious experience nor the struggle to live in a plural global village. In this book we speak from our own perspective as Christian religious educators, and our analysis provides a particular focus on the vocation of Christian churches in the education of the public. But we hope our redefinition of the role of the religious in education will continue to stimulate conversation among religious educators from a variety of faith communities about our common engagement in the midst of the public.

As we bring this project to a close, we are especially grateful to Donald Welch, president of Scarritt College, and to the college board of trustees for their vision of a graduate center in Christian education and church music, and for their invitation to join in the venture of developing its programs. We are also grateful to our wives, Janet Foster, Mary Lou O'Gorman, and Martha Seymour, and to our children, for accepting the turmoil of being uprooted and located in a new community, for seizing their own new possibilities in creative and venturesome ways, and for providing support and encouragement. Special thanks go to our secretary, Barbara Hunter, for the competence and calmness she brings to our common tasks.

We thank, as well, our professors in the history of education—Lawrence A. Cremin, Vincent P. Lannie, Robert W. Lynn, Jonathan Messerli, and Robert Polk Thomson—for the high standards they set in teaching and research, their ability to illuminate contemporary issues through their investigation of the past, and their encouragement as we continue our own quests to discern implications for public policy in the history of education.

*Jack Seymour*
*Bob O'Gorman*
*Chuck Foster*

# C H A P T E R I

# The Church
# in the Education
# of the Public

IN 1869, delegates from Sunday school unions and denominations across the United States gathered in Newark, New Jersey, for the Third National Sunday-School Convention. The spirit of the meeting was one of celebration as attempts were made to heal the divisions of war and share developments in national Sunday school work. The keynote speaker, the Honorable Theodore Runyon of New Jersey, proclaimed to the assembly that the Sunday school was becoming a great institution, spreading Christian faith throughout the land and making persons Christians. He noted that it was no longer an adjunct to the church but was central to it. More important, it had proved to be a substantial "means of popular education," influencing all classes of society. He saw it as the "leaven of society."[1]

Runyon's words set the tone for the convention. During the previous two decades the Sunday school had become an agency of the church. After much controversy, church leaders had decided that the school on the sabbath was to be the primary means of education for its people. No longer a benevolent school for the poor, it had become the church's school, and the hope for a literate Christian people was on its shoulders.

Yet despite the celebration of the Sunday school's coming

of age, several delegates were critical of the new developments. They felt impelled to warn the assembly that the public mission and educational heritage of the Sunday school must not be lost. Previously, the Sunday school had been a church's primary means of influencing the formation of the young in society. Many had been educated in reading, mathematics, morality, religion, and Christian citizenship within the walls of the Sunday school. While the critics wanted to celebrate the "new day" for the Sunday school, they did not want to lose its "public" purpose.

Their fear was made apparent in a session led by the nationally famous pastor of Pilgrim Congregational Church in Brooklyn, New York, Henry Ward Beecher. He preached that it was the responsibility of every church to found mission Sunday schools in which the original educative purposes would still be embodied. Reflecting on his own church's ministry at Bethel Mission Sunday School, which provided medical and legal counsel as well as library facilities and instruction, Beecher proclaimed that the church would lose its opportunity to be a voice in the city if it did not "provide for the instruction and education of the poor and outcast."[2] He believed that the church was obligated to be involved in the formation of the public.

> It is the part and right of every true Christian, in Christ's name, to subdue to the reign of truth, of justice, and of love, our whole land, but especially those parts of our land which represent intelligence and wealth and the civic power; and it is a crying sin upon our civilization and upon our Christianity, that to so large an extent, our great cities are dens of ignorance and lairs of iniquity.[3]

And the most practical way for the church to effect this evangelization, he reasoned, was to continue mission Sunday school work.

The delegates, both lay and clergy, received his words with applause and promises of commitment; at the same time, they were working to build the Sunday school into the church's school. Most did not perceive the tension Beecher sensed. For them it was now enough that the church had found a strategy for education.

Beecher's fear was that if Sunday school leaders forgot their responsibility to the poor and others outside the church, the moral influence of the church on society would be lost. His fear seems to have been perceptive because the public concerns of the Sunday school were replaced by church concerns. Before even ten years had passed, mission Sunday school work was no longer a major agenda. The church was so busy deciding how to organize classes for the instruction of its own people and determining the shape of an interdenominational Bible curriculum that mission schools became secondary. Church leaders knew the extent of the work needed to fulfill their own agenda of making the Sunday school into "the nursery of the church."[4] No time was left for the old public agenda. Religious education was thus domesticated within the household of the faith.

This Sunday school story from the mid-1800s is illustrative of the change in the church's educational goals. While most church leaders of that time knew that the church's influence in education included much more than formal Sunday school settings—things such as colleges, revivals, rallies, periodicals, and benevolent projects—their energy was expended primarily on the church's internal processes of education. The result was a narrowing of the self-understanding of the task of Christian education, an understanding that has continually restricted the church's education to the church itself. The effects of this domestication are pervasive throughout the last century in Christian religious education.

## The Domestication of Church Education

Our story of the relationship of church education to the education of the public begins in New England. Many colonists arrived there with the dream of embodying their Christian faith on American soil. To them the only proper way of life was religious. God's presence was real, and God's will for social life was reflected in their interpretations of the biblical tradition. Therefore daily life and religious life were to be coextensive. They covenanted to be God's community.

Of course, all the colonists could not agree about religious faith, and consequently the number of covenant communities multiplied as a result of religious interpretation, intolerance, and migration. These church leaders, who were also the political leaders of the new society, realized the central importance of education in their vision of public life. Education would protect them from the barbarism of the New World and also provide a means to ensure religious orthodoxy. Schools were therefore founded for both civilizing and religious purposes. In fact, one of the central precepts in the forming of the first colonial college, Harvard, emphasized religion as the foundation of learning and livelihood:

> Let every student be plainly instructed, and earnestly pressed to consider well, the main end of his life and studies is, to know God and Jesus Christ which is eternal life, Joh. 17:3, and therefore to lay Christ in the bottom, as the only foundation of all sound knowledge and learning.[5]

Complementing its interest in schools, the colonial scheme of education also included other agencies. The church reached out into all life affairs, becoming the hub of the educational efforts that formed people in the community of the New World. Lawrence Cremin, a historian of education in the United States, described this role:

> As has been indicated, the churches continued to serve as centers of instruction, both formal and informal, with ministers preaching, catechizing, and tutoring at every level; visiting the homes of parishioners on matters of doctrine and discipline;

itinerating as missionaries to the unconverted of every color and creed; writing books, pamphlets, tracts, and treatises on every conceivable topic, from ethics to iron mining; and in general carrying a host of *ad hoc* responsibilities that could range on any given day from passing on the fitness of prospective schoolteachers to prescribing for a pain in the stomach. Children learned to read in church by learning to repeat the catechism, and adults sharpened their political opinions while debating issues of Scripture. And all who joined in the fellowship of a like-minded congregation were in turn shaped by the standards of conduct and belief in that congregation, willy-nilly.[6]

For the "covenant community," then, the church was the center of the society. It affected civic life, the arts, and the propagation of public meanings. The church's educational task was pivotal to the formation and maintenance of society as a whole.

After the Revolution, with national growth, pluralism, and independence, a new educational strategy supplanted that of the covenant community. The founding documents of the United States explicitly protected society from the heteronomy of any one religious tradition. Churches, though, continued to have an important social function. Most founders agreed that religion provided the essential basis of a moral society. The church's public function took the form of moral proclamations, educational agencies, and benevolent activities which sought to describe the purpose of human life in God's unfolding history. During the late eighteenth and the nineteenth century, therefore, the church was one of several agencies necessary for society's maintenance. Through efforts such as Sunday schools for poor and frontier children, church-sponsored day schools in the cities, and church-related colleges, the church formally involved itself in the emerging educational efforts of the nation. Moreover, the benevolent activities—from temperance to abolition to care of orphans, to name a few—were directed toward educating the society into a pattern of life that would ameliorate social ills.

The church could no longer prescribe social organization, as had been true in some of the colonies. Voluntarism became an inescapable social reality, since religious liberty, protected in the Constitution and reflected in the public ethos, prohibited the church from either expecting to or being able to enforce religious uniformity. Therefore church life was characterized by free choice—individuals chose whether to join the church and cooperate for common causes. It was even necessary for congregations and denominations to join together voluntarily for common projects and social causes. Identification with the church became a matter of the "will to belong." Primary considerations were that individuals' needs be met through the church, that a person associate with his or her own kind, and that decisions be made through patterns of consensus.[7]

This spirit of voluntarism, however, provided the means for the church to expand and flourish in the new social context. It also increased the church's sensitivity to education. For the church to fulfill its role in moral influence, persons must first be recruited into the church and the message of the church must be widely disseminated. Thus church education became a means of gathering members and influencing their living.

As the church historian Martin Marty has indicated, Protestants, through much of the nineteenth century, sought to create a "righteous empire"—one that would allow the church "to attract the allegiance of all the people, to develop a spiritual kingdom, and to shape the nation's ethos, mores, manners, and often its laws." Although the rhetoric of church leaders and church educators focused on the connection between church work and civilization, in practice, the church's actual ability to affect this nation's civilization directly had diminished. It was now necessary for churches to concentrate their educational efforts on gathering members, and their influence on society was carried out either through those members or through voluntary amelioration societies. Marty argues rightly that this strategy boxed churches in, caused them to focus on their own internal life, and "practically and ideologically excluded [them] from major areas of public moral and ethical decision."[8] Moreover, Roman Catholics were excluded from the Protestant "righteous empire." The Catholic Church was forced to develop an educational strategy to form and maintain its own membership over against the Protestant ethos, to create its own public within the larger society.

Throughout the latter part of the nineteenth century and into the early twentieth, Protestant rhetoric blindly continued to reflect an educational agenda committed to shaping citizens. The comment of John Searles, Jr., a member of the executive committee of the Second International Sunday School Convention, is only one example of a much repeated conviction:

> There has been a steadily increasing respect for, and appreciation of, the Sunday-school not only in the church . . . but amongst thinking men *outside* the church. It is recognized as the agency on which more than any other we are to depend for Bible-loving citizens who are to stand for the defense of Protestantism and the dearest institutions of our republic.[9]

But practically, the church turned inward to maintain itself in the society. It emphasized church life. The mission Sunday school, as we have seen, was replaced by the church's Sunday school for its own members.

The educational task of the church, which in the colonial period had been to embody social life and meanings, in the national period became the gathering of members and the nurturing of the children of those members. The conversations of church educators immediately after the First World War illustrates this domestication. They wondered whether church education was effective at all. It had seemed to make little difference in protecting the world from war or youth from decadence. One church leader blamed what he called the "current moral crisis of youth" on the church's difficulty in dealing with the social disintegration following the war. The church, he concluded, must improve its educational program.[10]

The rhetoric of church education leaders concerning citizenship and public life continued. Character education in the 1920s, outrage at the atrocities of World War II, and present efforts at education for peace and justice are all examples. Yet the real question is one of strategy: How will the church contribute to the education of the public when its educational efforts are centered within the church, to gather members and nurture them and their children? This is the situation and the issue for contemporary Christian religious education.

Church education seems to have been domesticated to the household of the faithful, and religion itself seems to have been restricted to the arena of personal faith. The role the church can play in shaping the character of a citizen seems significantly reduced. And church education itself seems so interested in teaching the doctrines of the church and in helping people in their individual lives that the mission of the church in society is peripheral.[11]

Past strategies of church education have seemed to separate the church from the public world. Christian educators either have thrown their total energies into improving the church's efforts, or they have minimized the church's effect on education. One present assessment illustrates this either/or. Gabriel Moran, an important contemporary religious educator, has argued that there should be two types of educators in religion: (1) the church minister of education who works within the church to build its program of education, and (2) the religious educator proper, who is a professional, not holding a church office, and who works freed "from many of the limitations of ecclesial structures."[12] The first devotes his or her life to the church community, while the second works in the public arena to affect all education by stimulating the religious interplay of family, job, free time, and schooling. Even here, in a very provocative analysis, education for the church and religious education in the public are placed in conflict. Moran proposes a significant way to understand the relationship of religion to the spheres of life. He is aware of the domestication of church education, but assumes that religious educators need to move outside church control in order to protect themselves from that domestication.

In contrast, our own judgment reflects convictions held by Protestants Horace Bushnell and George Albert Coe, and by Catholics James H. Ryan and Bishop John Ireland, all pivotal minds in religious education: The church and the public cannot be separated. They are not substances to be dichotomized. The church and religion are rather part of the public, always influencing the public, and it is necessary for the church to understand this participation and to claim it.

Our thesis is that faith communities are the only intentional agencies within the public that have primary responsibility for the religious. For the church to restrict its educational ministry to itself ignores this crucial public responsibility. As Coe once argued, society will hear of religion from the church or not at all.[13] The churches must seek to understand their place within the total system of United States education, and they must seek to fulfill it. The church needs to hear again Theodore Runyon's proclamation to the Third National Sunday-School Convention: The church has in its hands a substantial "means of popular education." It is the "leaven of society."[14] The faith community must be the yeast in the larger community.

It is our conviction that this recognition is indeed possible if the church expands its own definition of education, if it seeks to understand how educational forces in the culture inter-relate, and if it attempts to work within that system of interrelationships. The task is one of church education—not narrowly defined only as education for the church, but also as education of the public. The church institutionally and ideologically has a public role in our culture. Martin Marty, for example, argues that a public church already exists. He is convinced that we only need to see it and to empower the connections within it. To use his words, "The public church does not await invention but discovery. When its participants recognize its scope, they can better realize their possibilities both individually and as a community."[15] We extend Marty's argument to church education. The relationship between church education and the formation of the people does not await invention, for it is already present and possible. What it awaits is discovery and commitment.

To that end, in this volume we explore the boundaries of the strategy of education in the United States and the place of the church in it. This is done through both contemporary analysis and a historical understanding of the relation of the church to the public in the formative periods of Protestant and Catholic education. For Protestants, two periods are addressed: (1) the Sunday school strategy of the middle-nineteenth century when the basic form of Protestant education was set; and (2) the reform period of the progressive church school in the first decades of the twentieth century, when the formal field of religious education and the profession "director of religious education" were born.[16] For Catholics, the nineteenth-century birth of the parochial school and its twentieth-century developments are crucial for understanding the formation of church strategies of education in the United States. Our analysis will provide a historical review of the church's vocation in the education of the public, through a critique of the domestication of church education and an exposition of the contemporary gaps in the education of the public that can be addressed only within a religious dimension.

## The Education of the Public

Bernard Bailyn shocked the field of education and expanded it significantly in his 1960 essay on the role of education in the formation of the United States. A colonial historian himself, Bailyn approached the issue as one that transcends the institution of the school. For him the basic issue was that civilization had been transmitted from Europe, particularly Great Britain, and that it had taken root on American soil. Bailyn knew that schools had played a role in the education and formation of these people, but he also knew that they were formed primarily through commerce, the arts, political life, media, churches, and publications. He demonstrated that *education* is a broader concept than *schooling*—it is *enculturation,* "the entire process by which culture transmits itself across the generations."[17]

Bailyn's notion expanded the view of what education includes and how culture maintains and transforms its lifeways over time. However, Bailyn's definition is so broad that it loses practical utility. Of course culture has always been transmitted through enculturation, but education is only part of that process—the intentional attempt to teach—and takes place only in those purposeful areas where educators can see their tasks and fulfill them. Lawrence Cremin preserved Bailyn's latitudinarian concept, but in his definition of education, which is now commonly accepted, restricted it to the intentional transmission of a culture: "the deliberate, systematic, and sustained effort to transmit, evoke, or acquire knowledge, attitudes, values, skills, and sensibilities, as well as any outcomes of that effort."[18]

These definitions suggest that education fundamentally deals with the way a culture mediates its substance and character and that its form consists of an ecology of interrelated institutions. The substance and character of a culture, which constitutes the content of education, Cremin calls the *paideia*. Reclaiming the ancient Greek word, he focuses on the fact that each culture has a dynamic "vision of life itself as a deliberate cultural and ethical aspiration."[19] It is this vision, drawn from the traditions and experiences of a people, that is the essential content of education. For example, the question for education in the United States is a question of the kind of people we want to form—the skills, values, aspirations, story, and feelings we want to embody. Education, then, is not only a technical issue—the transferring of skills from one generation to another—but the dynamic process of defining what is crucial to a people's life together. For Cremin, the colonial experience in the United States was primarily the transplanting of the paideia of an English village, summarized in the values of piety, civility, and learning.[20] This foundation powered the struggle of the independent nation to secure its own identity. In the national period, a distinctive stance on education was born "to advance a popular paideia compounded of democratic hopes, evangelical pieties, and millennial expectations."[21] This "American" vernacular was concerned with virtue, patriotism, and practical wisdom. It is this paideia, then, that still informs our conversations amidst competing economic realities, ethnic pluralism, and bureaucratic social organization.

Throughout the history of the education of the public in the United States, religion has been a significant component. It is the task of all education to mediate a heritage in the midst of contemporary experience. Every educator or educational agency struggles to discover: "What knowledge should 'we the people' hold in common? What values? What skills? What sensibilities?"[22] As these questions are being asked, the role of religion in the paideia is, in fact, being articulated.

Furthermore, the strategy by which paideia is mediated is

defined by Cremin as a configuration (or ecology) of educational institutions. In any age, the task of the educator is to think comprehensively about the institutions that seek to mediate culture, to think relationally about how these institutions fit into an educational matrix, and to think publically about the value of the education they mediate.[23] Families educate—as do workplaces, churches, schools, libraries, media, museums, and so on. It is imperative to recognize the educative agencies, as well as their connections. Cremin argues:

> Each of the major educative agencies performs a mediative role with respect to the others and with respect to society at large. . . . What is more, these various institutions mediate the culture in a variety of pedagogical modes and through a range of technologies for the recording, sharing, and distributing of symbols. In effect, they define the terms of effective participation and growth in the society.[24]

During the colonial period, then, household, church, and school stood in relation to one another, with the church at the center of education and life. With independence and the birth of a distinctive national character, the educational configuration united the symbols of Protestant Christianity with those of the nation, propagating them with equal and related power through families, churches, schools, rallies, and media. Today the configuration includes larger roles for entertainment, commerce, and voluntary associations, but many of the educational patterns of the national period remain strong.[25] For education to be defined, the range of institutions and their interrelationships need to be discerned. Therefore the task of the church educator is to determine the potential role of the church in this matrix and seek to fulfill it; otherwise church education will continue to be domesticated within the church and separated from "public education."

## The Church in the Education of the Public:
## A Preliminary Proposal

The educational structures that form the people in the United States, as well as the content of these structures, have changed significantly since the founding of the New England colonies. No longer is the church at the center of both the social and educational processes, and no longer is the covenant community or the righteous empire an image of social organization. Since the founding of this nation the relationship between the churches' educational ministries and the public order has continued to change. For the first one hundred fifty years the church, particularly the Protestant church, had a central role in the definition of the understanding of the nation and its life and mores. Although still significant, during the last fifty years this relationship has become more ambiguous. In this new situation, therefore, it is important for the church to understand the role it has played—how it both shaped public life and provided a religious support for cultural understandings, how it continues to function as an element within the nation's educational ecology, and how it can reinterpret its role and effect, particularly in relationship to social transformation for more humane and open structures for living.

The church historian Sidney Mead continues to remind the church of its integral relationship to this country's history when he calls the United States a "nation with the soul of a church."[26] The church has played a crucial and formative role in the development of the national character, not only by being an important teacher of the young, but by providing many of the images and visions that shaped peoples' understanding of human life and organization. During much of the nineteenth century, the church provided a rationale for directions in public policy. This was so much the case that the public schools functioned as Protestant parochial schools well

26

into the twentieth century. Although Roman Catholics, in turn, felt that a private system of education was essential to maintain their religious identity, their schools also functioned as "public schools," integrating their members into the public.

Since the founding of the United States, a pervasive issue has been the nurture of a common public life in the midst of pluralism. As leaders have sought ways to unite disparate groups into a common, democratic, humane people, to build commonality in the midst of new immigrants and new knowledge, they have always seen education as a primary vehicle for this unity. In the writings of Benjamin Rush, Horace Mann, and John Dewey, a vision of the role of education in the formation of the public life was clearly developed.[27] Yet beneath this vision has also been the conviction that religion was a crucial element in common life.

The significance of the historic role of church education is probably articulated nowhere as strongly as in the writings of both Protestant and Roman Catholic progressive religious educators in the first decades of the twentieth century when they sensed their influence eroding. They were convinced that their discipline and profession provided a context for addressing issues of public policy and common life. Roman Catholics such as James H. Ryan, who saw the democracy of the United States as infused with religious ideals, argued that Catholic schooling was essential to see that religious and moral ideas influenced the education of citizens.[28] Protestants like Henry F. Cope, the secretary of the Religious Education Association, stated the relationship correspondingly:

> Only the short-sighted can speak of the separation of religion and education. They are not two separate things which we must somehow harmonize; they are related as thought and action, as are life and feeling. . . . All true education is religious in the degree that it realizes the possibilities of persons growing in social fullness; all religion is educational in that it moves lives out into the realization of social destiny.[29]

27

Both major Christian faith communities sought to reclaim the religious roots of national life, at the same time focusing so heavily on the tasks of intrachurch life and education that they assured the continuation of the domestication of church education.

Recent experiences have shown the results of these strategies. With increased pluralism and secularization, the role of the church has increasingly diminished and become privatized. While there is no question that it continues to have a role, the church has had to struggle to understand the amount of influence it can have and to convince its own members that a public role is appropriate for it and for its education. Even those who have sought to respond to the new situation have tended to ignore the role of church education in the wider ecology. Instead, educators have turned to private schooling to create a comprehensive Christian environment for the young; or they have limited the church school to religious matters; or they have given up the idea that church education should turn to political action; or they have sought to extend the church's role in public schooling.

The church is therefore confronted with questions: Where does the church's educational ministry engage the ecology today? What are its agents and approaches? What are its concrete effects? All would probably agree that most education—even religious education—takes place through cultural socialization and therefore is affected by privatism and secularity.

If our reflections are correct, we are at a critical juncture in the history of both church education and public education. A new paideia, in relation to the older paideia of citizenship, democracy, and community is emerging, and the configuration of educational institutions is being re-formed. The church can play a significant role in this reformulation. As Martin Marty has argued, an awareness of "a *res publica,* the public order that surrounds and includes the people of faith" is

28

needed.[30] He identifies a potential convergence among the Protestant "mainline," the Roman Catholic, and the evangelical Christians which may initiate the recovery of a public conscience in the church. Such a public church, while accepting the need for religious and social pluralism, may empower a discovery of the task of the church amidst society.

Therefore Christian religious education needs to become aware of its role in today's wider educational ecology. The nature of education and of religion, and their relationship, needs to be rethought. Education must be broadly seen in its variety of cultural manifestations, religion must be seen as the possibility for infusing transcendence into cultural life, and church education must be seen at the intersection of the cultural images and religious images that form persons and cultural life. Approaches are needed to enable church education to provide religious education in the midst of the culture's education.

### The Church and Educational Paideia

Therefore let us, in a preliminary fashion, look at the emerging possibilities for an educational paideia and an educational strategy for church and public. Generations always seek to maintain a vision for human life and its mores, values, and sensibilities. In the midst of an era of change, the accepted paideia is of course challenged, but it may also provide a foundation for the birth of the new. Culture is never merely static, or it dies. When dynamic, a culture transforms itself in light of history and contemporary experience.

In our day it is not enough merely to maintain the past. A commitment to pluralism as different vantage points on truth and meaning, to the global village as the only arena that allows for the survival of human life, and to the resolving of many of the crucial social problems that affect the human future— these demand in turn an education that is committed to the values of personhood (child of God) and community (shalom) and is open to the building of humane patterns of social life.

James W. Botkin, Mahdi Elmandjra, and Mircea Malitza, in their report to the Club of Rome on education, claim that at present there is a human gap between the actual consequences of human action on the environment, and the recognition of the consequences of those actions in the future. Learning is the vehicle for responding to this gap by preparing people to enter the actual construction of the new: "For us, learning means an approach, both to knowledge and to life, that emphasizes human initiative. It encompasses the acquisition and practice of new methodologies, new skills, new attitudes, and new values to live in a world of change." Therefore learning must extend beyond the institution of schooling and the traditional practices of education committed primarily to maintenance. It must not be limited to the cognitive grasp of data; it must also excite and facilitate the creation of images for reshaping people and their environment, thereby providing new institutional interrelationships which promote anticipation of the future and participation in its construction. It will need to integrate individual and societal learning as well as cognitive and imaginal learning; root itself in the multiple contexts of life which mediate meanings; and restore values, human relationships, and images and visions as central to the educational process.[31] In such a manner educational strategies develop from the contexts in which people find meaning, and thus these strategies directly address the issues so important for a global future.

The historic paideia that was the vernacular of public education in the United States, and the variety of human contexts such as churches, voluntary associations, and ethnic heritages that contributed to this vision—all are crucial to the formation of a new learning content focused on bridging the human gap. This is precisely what Cremin meant when he argued that education must be addressed publically. Without a full participatory exploration into the parts of a culture that are to be taught and the way they are to be taught, education remains in the realm of maintenance and avoids transformation. Educators need to ask how their work is to be done in the midst of a society of plural meanings and plural institutions. Cremin states the agenda with passion and poetry:

> In the last analysis, the fundamental mode of politics in a democratic society is education, and it is in *that* way over all others that the educator is ultimately projected into politics. What is apparent here is the ancient prophetic role which Dewey himself had in mind when he wrote in 1897 that the teacher is always "the prophet of the true God" and "the usherer in of the true kingdom of God." . . . Prophesy: in its root meaning, the calling of a people, via criticism and affirmation, to their noblest traditions and aspirations. Prophesy, I would submit, is the essential public function of the educator in a democratic society.[32]

The church is as much an arena in this public discussion as are commerce and media. It was an essential part of the formation of the paideia, and it is part of the prophetic role of education to link tradition and aspiration artistically and politically.[33] Not only *is* there a public church, but there *must* be, if this educational agenda is to be fulfilled.

### The Church in the Educational Ecology

The role of the church is even more clearly visible when we turn to an analysis of the ecology of education in the United States. Not only is the paideia in transition, but the educational ecology is in a period of significant change, and public educators who understand its dynamics are aware of these profound changes. The predominant ecology set during the latter half of the nineteenth century is shifting as the

31

economy changes from industrial to high technology/ information processing. Herman Niebuhr, Jr., the associate vice-president of Temple University, says that educational ecology in the United States is entering a watershed period—a "once-in-a-century update."[34]

Niebuhr's term for the ecology is "human learning system." With the proliferation of methods of intentional individualized instruction; with the many peer groups for leisure, at work, or in associations; with the increase of media; and with the decrease in traditional structures of authority, Niebuhr argues that the mainline components of educational ecology— higher education, the family, the community, religious institutions, schools, media, and workplaces—all need adjustment. The institutional awareness of the role of each and of the ability of each to strengthen the system is necessary, as well as a reorientation of the clientele of each to its wider educational responsibilities and an increased networking across institutions within the ecology.[35] It may now be possible to build an ecology for education intentionally, rather than merely letting it emerge as we did in the late nineteenth century. In fact, if one accepts the notion of a human gap in learning, it is imperative to do so.

As the ecology was being formed throughout the last two centuries, the church played a crucial role in educational configurations. The church again has an opportunity and a responsibility to be involved in the emerging ecology. In *To Empower People,* Peter Berger and John Richard Neuhaus describe the church as carrying the potential for contributing to the vision that empowers education and to the system that is effected. They argue that today the church has the crucial sociological role of mediating between persons and public policy, that modernization produces a dichotomy between public and private spheres of life.[36] In previous eras people could see their influence on public policy because of the human scale of institutions, political processes, and economic organization; modernization, on the other hand, produces megastructures. Big labor, big business, big government, and big education are examples of these megastructures and their bureaucratic organizations. Individuals are separated from the public processes which formerly gave life meaning, and they are forced to find fulfillment in the private sphere of life. The result is that individual meaning tends to become idiosyncratic and precarious. Choice is proliferated, personal anomie results, and the democratic political process is questioned.

However, Berger and Neuhaus argue that several institutions can function as mediating structures to connect the personal to the public. These structures

> have a private face, giving private life a measure of stability, and they have a public face, transferring meaning and value to the megastructures. . . . Their strategic position derives from their reducing both the anomic precariousness of individual existence in isolation from society and the threat of alienation to the public order.[37]

The neighborhood, the family, the church, and voluntary associations are the four predominant mediating structures in the public life of the United States. It is the action of these and other such structures that is essential in forming and connecting public meanings and making democratic life possible. The particular intermediary roles of these institutions is thus crucial.

The role of the church is particularly significant. Though many of its functions have been privatized, the church still functions to legitimate personal meanings and values and to provide the public realm with central symbols, stories, and visions. Berger and Neuhaus continue:

> Not only are religious institutions significant "players" in the public realm, but they are singularly important to the way

people order their lives and values at the most local and concrete levels of their existence. Thus they are crucial to understanding family, neighborhood, and other mediating structures of empowerment.[38]

The church, then, as our thesis suggests, is the yeast in the public order. Faith communities function as intentional agencies within the public and have primary responsibility for the way the religious infuses both personal and public life. The church is called to discern and point to the presence of the transcendent in human life and to provide the means for reconstructing all of life in relation to a religious dimension.

Therefore the church's educational ministry extends far beyond internal educational programming to crucial questions about what parts of the culture are to be transmitted and transformed, and how. While the particular role of the church has lessened, it is without question still a partner in the public discussion of education for the forming of a people, and it contributes to the formation of the public paideia.

Our hope, in these chapters, is to describe the role church education has played in the forming of the public of the United States and to reveal missed opportunities and lost visions. We aim to reveal a clear commitment to the public and to find appropriate strategies for church educators. Perhaps this commitment can be effected in our time, amidst our own visions and missed opportunities, as the role of the church in the ecology of the United States is intentionally recovered.

### Notes

1. Theodore Runyon, "The Address of Welcome," in *The Third National Sunday-School Convention of the United States 1869* (Philadelphia: J. C. Garrigues & Co., 1869), p. 7.
2. Henry Ward Beecher, "The Mission Work of the Sunday School," in *Third National Sunday-School Convention,* p. 69.
3. Ibid.
4. For a full discussion, see Anne M. Boylan, "'The Nursery of the Church':

Evangelical Protestant Sunday Schools, 1820–1880" (Ph.D. diss., University of Wisconsin, 1973).

5. "New England's First Fruits," in Samuel E. Morison, *The Founding of Harvard College* (Cambridge: Harvard University Press, 1935), p. 434. I have used contemporary spelling in the quotation.

6. Lawrence A. Cremin, *American Education: The Colonial Experience, 1607–1783* (New York: Harper & Row, 1970), pp. 493-94.

7. For a fuller treatment of the issue of voluntarism, see D. B. Robertson, ed., *Voluntary Associations: A Study of Groups in Free Societies* (Richmond: John Knox Press, 1966), esp. essays by Robert Handy and James Gustafson.

8. Martin E. Marty, *Righteous Empire: The Protestant Experience in America* (New York: Dial Press, 1970), foreword and p. 77.

9. John E. Searles, Jr., "Report of the Executive Committee," in *Second International Sunday-School Convention of the United States and British American Provinces* (Washington, D.C.: Executive Committee, 1878), p. 20.

10. Ernest Thomas, "The Current Moral Crisis for Youth," *Religious Education* 16 (April 1921):76-80.

11. See Langdon Gilkey, *Catholicism Confronts Modernity: A Protestant View* (New York: Seabury Press, 1975), p. 14. Gilkey argues that Protestantism became "so engulfed in that [United States] world as merely to reproduce the individualistic, quantitative, moralistic, nonemotional, and in many respects naturalistic, bourgeois world in ecclestiastical form."

12. Gabriel Moran, *Interplay: A Theory of Religion and Education* (Winona, Minn.: St. Mary's Press, 1981), p. 96.

13. George Albert Coe, "The President's Annual Address: New Reasons for Old Duties," *Religious Education* 5 (April 1910):4.

14. See n. 1.

15. Martin E. Marty, *The Public Church: Mainline—Evangelical—Catholic* (New York: Crossroads Publishing Co., 1981), p. 3.

16. For a description of the domestication of progressive religious education, see Stephen A. Schmidt, *A History of the Religious Education Association* (Birmingham: Religious Education Press, 1983).

17. Bernard Bailyn, *Education in the Founding of American Society* (New York: W. W. Norton & Co., 1960), p. 14.

18. Lawrence A. Cremin, *Public Education* (New York: Basic Books, 1976), p. 27.

19. Lawrence A. Cremin, *Traditions of American Education* (New York: Basic Books, 1977), p. 19.

20. Ibid., p. 12.

21. Ibid., p. viii.

22. Cremin, *Public Education*, p. 74.

23. Ibid., pp. 57-77.

24. Ibid., pp. 22-23.

25. See Cremin's brief overview of history in *Traditions of American Education* or his comprehensive treatment in *American Education: The Colonial Experience* and *American Education: The National Experience 1783–1876* (New York: Harper & Row, 1980).

26. Sidney E. Mead, *The Nation with the Soul of a Church* (New York: Harper & Row, 1975).

27. E.g., see Rush's comments in *A Plan for the Establishment of Public Schools and the Diffusion of Knowledge in Pennsylvania; to Which Are Added Thoughts upon the Mode of Education, Proper in a Republic. Addressed to the Legislature and Citizens of the State* (Philadelphia: Thomas Dobson, 1786): "The only useful foundation for a useful education in a republic is to be laid in *Religion*. Without this there can be no virtue, and without virtue there can be no liberty, and liberty is the object and life of all republic governments." Also see *The Republic and the Schools: Horace Mann on the Education of Free Men*, ed. Lawrence A. Cremin (New York: Bureau of Publications, Teachers College, Columbia University, 1957); John Dewey, *A Common Faith* (New Haven: Yale University Press, 1934).

28. James H. Ryan, "Religious Education and Democracy," *Catholic Education Review* 21 (June 1923).

29. Henry F. Cope, *Education for Democracy* (New York: Macmillan Co., 1920), p. 82.

30. Marty, *Public Church*, p. 3.

31. James W. Botkin, Mahdi Elmandjra, and Mircea Malitza, *No Limits to Learning: Bridging the Human Gap* (Oxford: Pergamon Press, 1979), pp. 6-9 (quote, p. 8). Also see discussion, pp. 17-44.

32. Cremin, *Public Education*, pp. 76-77.

33. Ibid., p. 96, citing Whitehead and Dewey.

34. Herman Niebuhr, Jr., "Strengthening the Human Learning System," *Change* 14 (November/December 1982):16-21; and "Strategies and Technologies for Higher Education to Meet Industry Training Needs in the 80s: A Once-in-a-Century Update of the Model," paper presented to Fifth National Conference on Communications and Technology in Education and Training, March 1983.

35. Niebuhr, "Human Learning System," pp. 19-20.

36. Peter L. Berger and Richard John Neuhaus, *To Empower People: The Role of Mediating Structures in Public Policy* (Washington, D.C.: American Enterprise Institute for Public Policy Research, 1977), pp. 1-4.

37. Ibid., p. 3.

38. Ibid., p. 26.

# Christian and Voluntary: Education in a Nineteenth-Century Protestant Public

HORACE Bushnell had no doubts about the role and function of the church or of the clergy in the public sector. In a sermon preached at the height of the "commotion of the popular spirit" that was heaving the "bosom of the nation" during the presidential campaigns of Harrison (of Tippecanoe and Tyler Too fame) and Van Buren, Bushnell reminded his congregation of his responsibilities as a "minister of religion" to "search out what is morally corrupt or dangerous" and "assert the laws of God," that they might establish their "sober influence" over the minds and actions of the populace.[1] Four years later he again introduced an election year sermon by typically claiming, "I cannot let politics alone, till I am shown that politics are not under the government of God and beyond the sphere of moral obligation."[2]

Bushnell, along with many of his peers in the ministry, assumed the political implications of Christianity. Hence they saw no contradiction between their role as clergy and their forays into the moral principles of public issues. The public was the concern of the church, just as they perceived the church to be a constitutive part of the public. Nowhere was this fact more evident than in the attention many nineteenth-century Protestant Christians gave to the shaping of the national life through education. The educational historian David Tyack has made the same point. In a study of the role of clergy in the common school movement, he concluded that the founding of schools was "part of a pervasive Protestant crusade. Schools and churches were allies in the quest to create the Kingdom of God in America."[3]

Bushnell and his contemporaries perceived the nation to be at a critical point in its history. Expanding rapidly to the West, coping with the presence of a growing population of non-English-speaking immigrants, adapting to the shift from an agrarian to an urban culture in the Northeast, contending with the cancerous blight of slavery and the insidious treatment of the Native American—all contributed to a pervasive sense that the national destiny inherent in the nation's origins was being threatened. This realization heightened the efforts of nineteenth-century Protestant leaders to tame the wild, the alien, the barbarous elements in society and to incorporate the stranger and the newcomer into the national life and purpose.

From one perspective they were highly successful. In a relatively short period of time, the nation was covered by Sunday, public, and sectarian schools, colleges, and universities. Newspapers, literary societies, libraries, and later, the Chautauqua circuit, expanded the sphere of their influence. Our thesis, however, is that in spite of these successes, in their struggle to find an educational strategy congruent with their view of the national destiny, they underestimated both the radically diverse character of the United States public and the limitations of their strategy. The evidence of that failure did not become obvious until the twentieth century, when Protestant church leaders sought to alter the character of that commitment to education in order to accomplish the continuing goal of a Christian nation.

## Christian Educators: Agents of a Public Consciousness

In the latter half of the nineteenth century, those who envisioned education as a primary strategy for shaping the national character and destiny according to Christian principles were often called *Christian* educators. The phrase was a broad one, encompassing both clergy and laity and, in contrast to contemporary professional usage, described anyone who advocated the Christian education of the nation. In a meeting of "Christian Educators" in 1881, for example, the delegates heard lectures on a variety of public issues: illiteracy; national aid to common schools; the relationship of illiteracy, wealth, pauperism, and crime; and education in the South, as well as a series of lectures dealing with the education of Negroes, Indians, and Mormons. The concluding lecture series focused on "Christ in American Education." Speakers included clergy, religious editors, two black bishops from the African Methodist Episcopal Church, the United States Secretary of the Interior, the principal of a normal school in New York, the United States Commissioner of Education, a United States Senator, metropolitan newspaper editors, and lawyers. Although the overwhelming majority of speakers were men, two women spoke on topics related to their specific work.[4] This conference illustrates a viewpoint typical of the period. *Educators* were seen as those persons who advocated the advancement of the educational institutions of the nation. *Christian* described their ideological perspective on the educational task. They focused their efforts not upon the church itself, but upon the responsibility of the church to interpret and influence the life and work of the nation.

This commitment of evangelical Protestant leaders permeates their writings. Lyman Beecher's *Plea for the West* in 1835 set the tone for subsequent works and was often quoted to illustrate both their concern about the consequences that might result from the lack of civilizing influences in that region and their belief that education (schooling) could mold its future. Tyack's research conclusively illustrates the leading role of clergy in the founding of schools in the West. In the established East, clergy also took primary responsibility for advocating and supporting the common-school movement so often associated with Horace Mann and Henry Barnard.

Horace Bushnell, pastor of the growing middle-class North Congregational Church in Hartford, Connecticut, was a man of many talents. Having received the acclaim of his contemporaries as an outstanding preacher, an astute although controversial theologian, a popular lecturer for civic events, and an often perceptive social critic, he has been described as one of the more thoughtful and perceptive interpreters of the age by several historians of United States life and thought.[5] In theological circles he is best known as one of the more original and provocative theologians of the period. Religious educators, however, have tended to view his work through the eyes of the progressives of the early twentieth century, who often called him the "father of religious education" because he symbolized the break in the hold of conversion modalities on the religious education of children.[6] This symbolic role has kept his name in the history books, but the lack of an appropriate critical perspective on his work has limited our understanding of his contribution to the educational work of the church.

The breadth of Bushnell's commitment to education, however, may be seen in his involvement in local school activities, his advocacy of common-school reform, and his support of the many voluntary societies that made up the educational ecology of the period. He wrote extensively on such issues as the education of children, the symbolic and evocative nature of language, religion as the source of the moral character of a people, and the interdependence of religion and education in the development of that character. Bushnell did not approach these themes with the intention of contributing to educational thought, nor was he primarily interested in the education of the church. Instead he embodied an educational perspective in his approach to specific theological and social issues. He spoke for that broad segment of the mid-nineteenth-century population which assumed that education was the key to the formation of national identity and character.

In subsequent years the extent of Bushnell's educational views and commitments were domesticated by Sunday school educators who encapsulated them within the church. It is in the work of Henry Clay Trumbull, editor of *The Sunday School Times,* that we may most clearly discern the appropriation and popularization of Bushnell's views during the last half of the century. Trumbull acknowledged his indebtedness to Bushnell, especially for an understanding of nurture in the education of children, of the potential in the unconscious influence of Sunday school teachers in leading children to the love of Jesus, and of the limited but evocative character of language as a vehicle for communicating truth.[7]

It is in the contrast, however, between Bushnell's vision of the education of the public, shared by his peers, and the domestication of that vision in the work of Sunday school leaders like Trumbull, that we may begin to discern clues to the continuing quest for the interdependence of religion and education in the national life and the diminishing role of the church's education in the task of public formation.

## An Educational Ideology for the Church in the Public

Drawing upon the legacies of the Reformation with its emphasis on the sovereignty of God, the sinfulness of humanity, a personal accountability for one's relationship to God and to the world, and the covenant as the source of social bounds; and upon the Enlightenment with its emphasis on individual freedom, personal responsibility, and social contract, men and women of this period created "doctrines" which informed their sense of national identity and mission. Prominent among these doctrines were those contending that the United States was to be God's flag nation; its people, Christian patriots. These doctrines formed the substance of much of the social and political writing of Horace Bushnell and were adopted by many of the Sunday school leaders of the later nineteenth century.

Bushnell was of the opinion that a true sense of nationality occurred at that point in history when the "character" of a people finally demonstrated its loyalty to God in the national life. It depended not only upon the providence of God, but upon human response to the divine initiative.[8] With such a belief in God's guidance in the movement of history, Bushnell assumed that God also formed nations to embody some larger purpose in the course of human experience—that when God intended any great historic movement, "some flag nation" would be appointed to marshal and direct the nations of the world. That nation, with its own flag as the symbol of its "spiritual core," would "take the lead in an era and thus give bent to the world's thoughts, furnish ideas of pursuit," and "command its movements."[9] Bushnell shared the common conviction that the United States must have its own turn as a flag nation and that its contribution would be—indeed, already had been—dramatic and revolutionary. He contended that the movement, initiated by God through the obedience of the nation's ancestors and developed in the concept of self-government, meant the nation would stand, in Trumbull's words, "between the centuries" as the future hope of former ages.[10]

Bushnell believed the time had come for the United States to exercise its leadership in actualizing a sense of nationality "in the fires of history upon the evil of suffering under the manner of a Providential God."[11] His view of progress was tempered by his awareness of the presence of tragedy in the flow of history. Just as Christ had reconciled the world to God through his vicarious sacrifice, so the formation of societies relied on the sacrifice of men and women in events like the Civil War to achieve a sense of unity that would embody its national destiny. Hence the fundamental task of the nation centered on the development of public consciousness; the task of education, the shaping of public character.

Perhaps at no point does Bushnell more appropriately reflect the changing perspectives of the mid-nineteenth century than in his description of the role of the state under the authority of God in the formation of her citizenry. Optimism and a sense of progressivism marked his theological thought. He "carried the interpretation" of human agency "further than others," moreover, "by continuing to weaken the old doctrines of corruption and depravity." In this doctrine of "flag nation," Bushnell emphasized the role of human responsibility in fulfilling the national destiny. The prevalence of this belief meant that the typical nineteenth-century Protestant could neither "let unsaved men alone or let saved men go it alone."[12]

From this vantage point, therefore, the purpose of education was to elicit "the powers of youth to the highest degree possible," which meant being "formed to truth and virtue."[13] This emphasis clearly modified Bushnell's understanding of patriotism. He found fanaticism or blind allegiance offensive. Instead, patriotic citizens would insist upon justice, conscientious effort, moral uprightness—both in their own behavior and in that of their leaders. A patriotic citizen would act out of a sense of responsibility to God, both in his or her personal life and in the support of "good institutions."[14] Bushnell's emphasis upon education centered not upon the church, but upon the raising of Christian patriots, citizens of the United States whose polity and destiny, or purpose, would be wholly new among the nations.

Acknowledging their dependence upon the higher laws of

God, these Christian patriots would enact legislation as a sign of their allegiance to God. They would establish institutions such as common schools and universities as an expression of their concern for the unity and future godliness of the nation. They would select leaders who revealed an appreciation for and a willingness to work for the justice and righteousness of God. The social and legal life of a nation under God, in other words, would embody the higher laws of God.

To sum up, the ideological impetus for Bushnell's understanding of education was located in the mid-nineteenth-century view of the national destiny that had been formed in the Puritan visions of a society of people distinguished by their faithfulness and obedience to God. It claimed the interdependence of Christian commitment to God and national patriotism. And it emphasized the centrality of education in fulfilling the vision of the United States as the flag nation leading the world into a more just and moral future.

## A Voluntary Strategy for a Public Identity

In an early sermon on the common schools, Bushnell reminded his congregation that "education without religion, is education without virtue. Religion without education . . . is a cold, unpaternal principle, dying without propagation."[15] He emphasized that education was the noblest work of religion and concluded by urging his congregation to support the common schools of the state as a primary moral responsibility. Yet he never equated education with schooling, or religion with churches. Both were social functions inherent in human experience. They infused specific agencies with meaning and purpose.

Therefore the interdependence of religion and education is integral to Bushnell's strategy of shaping God's flag nation through Christian patriots. That strategy consisted of binding together school, church, and family through a common national context and a mutual allegiance to God. Together, these three agencies shared primary responsibility for shaping the national character and destiny. They functioned inter-dependently in the community, in contrast to the Puritan notion of the church as the foundation of that same strategy. Secondary in importance were the host of other voluntary societies, from the Sunday school to the vast number of tract, Bible, and missionary societies which supported and extended the efforts of the three agencies.

In this educational strategy Bushnell believed that the school was indispensable. It linked the diverse children of the community in a common experience, with the intention that they might become citizens with both public and Christian perspectives. He contended that the nation was no longer Puritan or Protestant, but "American," in the sense that it now included people who did not share the common features of either of these traditions. Bushnell observed that in the act of admitting and granting the right to vote to people who did not share that heritage, the nation had "slid off, impercepti-bly, from the Old Puritan, upon an American basis," undertaking, in the process, the inauguration of "a form of political order that holds no formal church connection."[16] Hence he shared with Horace Mann the vision that the common school provided the best way for people from all walks of life to mingle during their impressionable years, so that as they matured they might be united in "fraternal feelings" and thereby overcome the "alienating competi-tions" found in the social and economic distinctions of the adult world.[17]

By the mid-1850s, Bushnell no longer envisaged the common school as a Protestant institution. Indeed he even foresaw a time, especially in the heterogeneous cities, when the Bible could not be read in the schools because the translation might offend either Protestant or Catholic. But in his opinion, this trend would not necessarily remove either the Catholic or the Protestant basic Christian commitment to schools. He believed that formal religious instruction was not essential because more "real Christian truth" could be communicated to Catholic and Protestant children while they sat side by side, their conduct "regulated" by Christian teachers and administrators who lived according to the principles of "truth, order, industry, and obedience" laid upon their consciences by their own relationship to God.[18]

Bushnell looked upon the church as another agency of the community—one that particularly infused the community with its loyalty to Christ. The church ensured the presence of people whose participation in the public arena would reveal their obedience to God and create a "new supernatural order" of humanity, exalted with a higher sense of "truth, beauty, and weight of character."[19] These tasks in the United States had been well begun, but were far from complete. Bushnell apparently approved of the Sunday school as one limited agency of the church in education. The Sunday school was effective in mission settings, but he did not envision it as having a primary role in the education of the congregation. His attention was directed instead toward congregational education through the church's corporate life, located in common worship and attendance upon the preached world. In this regard, his ministerial leadership seemed more like that of his Puritan forebears than that of the newer style pastors, represented by his neighboring colleague Joel Hawes of Centre Church. While Bushnell's congregation did report a Sunday school, it lacked the size and vitality of Hawes' extensive system of classes and groups for all ages. For Bushnell, the church's strength existed in the faith of its members. If they were faithful, the church would naturally increase and extend its influence throughout the community and beyond into the world.

As the third agency in this educational strategy, the family linked the generations naturally by transmitting values, commitments, and behaviors inherited from the past. The family, in both conscious and unconscious ways, engaged in a moral effort to shape the character of the children in its midst. Although Bushnell believed in free will, he was also sensitive to what later sociologists would call the patterns of socialization. He observed that all members of the family, "locked together" in a common enterprise, "are trained by necessity" into behaviors and attitudes, much like stones "rolled together in some brook or eddy" by the force of the stream until "they wear each other into common shapes."[20]

The constellation of school, church, and family was certainly not original with Bushnell. The Puritans had asserted that interdependence long before. Bushnell, however, recast the oligarchical character of that ecology in his commitment to the principles of voluntarism, integral to his view of the character and destiny of the nation. Those principles significantly shaped his perception of the distinctive contribution of each of these three educational agencies.

Bushnell shared the popular view that education was not to be imposed politically. The public's education depended rather upon the voluntary goodwill of persons to seek out those relationships and agencies that would effectively introduce them into the values and practices of a Christian society. Their participation in family, church, and school would thereby elicit, through the natural influence of their common experience, a Christian culture. Thus the character of the nation would be shaped by people's loyalty to the principles for social order located in their faithfulness to God. Bushnell believed the unity of the nation would emerge out of mutual discovery of the distinctive contributions of the diverse elements in the population. It is in his discussion of the way loyalty centers a people around a common purpose, comprehensiveness gathers a diverse people into a common identity, and influence shapes the character of both individuals and groups in the common life of the nation, that we may discern Bushnell's commitment to voluntarism in the education of the public.

Bushnell once called loyalty a "volunteer devotion." Whether he understood it as such or not, his doctrine of loyalty is a voluntary concept. He found he could not define the legal or social structures integral to loyalty, but instead located its features in what people think, feel, and contrive—not from any command or sense of obligation, but of their "own accord"—for the country and the country's honor. It is "older than the constitution; a moral bond created by Disposing Providence, and sanctified to be the matrix of the coming nationality and the constitution to be."[21] It is in that little phrase, "of their own accord" that the distinctive character of the voluntaristic emphasis in Bushnell's view of loyalty becomes evident. James Gustafson points out that the shift is from *assenting* to the normative principles undergirding society, to *consenting* to them. It involves the willful alignment of oneself with those principles until they are evident in one's outlook and conduct. The responsibility for entrance into the social fabric of society lies with the individual who chooses to associate with the larger body.[22]

The dilemma for those who supported voluntary principles for social organization existed in the potential disruption in the relationship between older and younger generations. The transmission of older values, ideals, and commitments could not be assumed in the continuity of national traditions, but had to be appropriated and updated by each successive generation. The burden rested not upon the children and youth of the community, but upon their elders, who were their only link to the past. It was necessary that patterns of transmission be increasingly intentional and self-conscious for this mobile and increasingly diverse population. That dilemma was resolved by the Beechers, by Bushnell, Mann, and Barnard, and by the Sunday school leaders in their commitment to the education of the public through the school and in their extensive promotion of the common and Sunday schools as the most effective agencies for nurturing loyalty to the national traditions and visions that would produce Christian and patriotic citizens.

The voluntary nature of Bushnell's view of education is also evident in the principle of comprehensiveness he developed to guide the decisions of men and women faced by the ecclesiastical and, one might add, the social, economic, and cultural divisions of the day. Bushnell's understanding of comprehensiveness may be compared with the views of such voluntary agencies as the American Sunday School Union and the Evangelical Alliance. These groups located the unity of a people in the commonly held values and ideas. This perspective eliminated from cooperative work anything that might emphasize member differences or evoke controversy. In contrast, Bushnell viewed the task of inclusivity as one of discerning the distinctive contributions of all parties for the enrichment of the life of the whole. Actually, both approaches were based on voluntary assumptions for social organization. Each assumed that the associations of people depended upon the free choice of the members. Bushnell's theory was distinctive, however, because it began with an epistemological rather than a political concern. The primary issue for Bushnell centered on the limited grasp of truth on the part of any group of people. He assumed that truth did not change; people did. Since their "contents" and "antagonisms" differed for many reasons, he contended that people could not "see the same truths in the same forms."[23] The consequent problem for the structures of human community existed in the finite manner in which people couched and expressed their commitments, beliefs, and perceptions. Hence the comprehensiveness of a society depended upon its capacity to discern diverse perspectives on truth, conveyed by the language its members shared in common. Bushnell's theory of language provides the underpinnings for his theory of comprehensiveness. Influenced by Samuel Taylor Coleridge and by his teacher of Greek and Hebrew at Yale Divinity School, Josiah Willard Gibbs, Bushnell pushed beyond the dominant contemporary notion that language could fully embody truth. His theory begins with the assertion that truth is ultimately revealed only in God. Any human expression of truth must thereby be limited in both scope and content. Furthermore, language is a human invention, he believed and, as such, inherently limited.

One of Bushnell's more poignant reflections on the potential in a comprehensive perspective toward the education of the people of the nation is found in his sermon "Common Schools." His view of comprehensiveness reinforced the rhetoric of the common-school reformers, who envisioned the school as taking radically diverse peoples and, by their common life, shaping them into a new people. Acknowledging the contemporary pain precipitated by the contrary claims for the schools voiced by Protestant and Catholic, he brought his sermon to a close:

> Probably no existing form of Christianity is perfect: The Romish we are sure is not; the Puritan was not, else why should it so soon have lost its rigors? The Protestant more generally viewed, contains a wider variety of elements, but these too seem to be wanting for some process of assimilation that should weld them finally together. Therefore, God, we may suppose, throws all these diverse multitudes, Protestant and Catholic, together, in crossings so various, and a ferment of experience so manifold, that he may wear us into some other and higher and more complete unity than we are able, of ourselves and by our own wisdom, to settle. . . . [Perhaps our youth, through the schools] may learn how also to be no more strangers and foreigners, but fellow-citizens with the saints and of the household of God.[24]

In 1846 Bushnell first spelled out his understanding of "influence" in the education of people in a sermon preached at Fetters Lane Chapel in London. This discussion established the framework for his essays on nurture in the education of children, published the following year. He maintained that families, organizations, and nations could be distinguished, in part, from similar social organisms because of the effects of the distinctive unconscious influences at work in each body. This "common spirit" acted as a power that "interfused" the relationships of people, a "comprehensive will" that "actuated" a common character in a quite invisible manner.[25]

Forty years later, Henry Clay Trumbull would claim that "Bushnell did more than any man had done before, to bring out the importance and the practical value of this involuntary or unconscious influence."[26] Bushnell was not alone in his interest in the patterns of "involuntary" influence, as Ann Douglas makes clear in her important study of *The Feminization of American Culture.* She documents the decreasing power of clergy and women in the industrial cities of the Northeast and their growing reliance upon "moral and psychic nurture" to "influence" people in as unobtrusive and pervasive a manner as possible. Douglas has illustrated how the popular literature of the day became the primary means for exerting such influence. Women like Lydia Sigourney, a contemporary of Bushnell and also from Hartford, wrote dozens of stories designed to convey the values of feminine influence. Bushnell, along with Henry Ward Beecher, Noah Porter, and a host of other clergy, developed national reputations through the medium of the press. In her analysis of the period, Douglas concludes that women and clergy turned to "influence" to reclaim the power they were losing. In the process, both women and clergy "inevitably confused theology with religiosity, religiosity with literature, and literature with self-justification."[27]

In many ways Bushnell's discussion of the power of unconscious influence seems unrelated to this larger cultural perspective. His discussion is unabashedly theological. His thinking is often rigorous and anticipates the insights of the social psychologists and anthropologists of the twentieth century who discuss similar phenomena under the rubric of socialization theory. Compared with the notions of influence that dominated the popular novels and women's magazines of the period, Bushnell's theory of influence was anything but unobtrusive. Indeed, it sparked through all his essays on Christian nurture, one of the more virulent and vehement theological controversies of the period. (One of his more vocal critics, Bennet Tyler, simply labeled Bushnell's theory absurd.)

At the same time, it must be recognized that Bushnell's theory received a hearing partly because the refinement and propriety of these new and popular domestic notions provided an expressive antidote to the barbarism in the cities and in the West, which many feared might threaten the nation's cultural life. Bushnell systematized the concept and elevated it to a theoretical structure with the potential for guiding the religious and moral development of a family, a congregation, even a nation. Again influenced by the insights of the Romanticists, especially Coleridge, and his own powers of observation, Bushnell discerned, in a manner alien to many of his peers, the pervasive power of nonrational elements in the human experience to shape the lives of children and youth.

In his original essay Bushnell identified three social experiences, each rooted in the volitional element of human nature that "influences" values, commitments, and behavior: the child's instinctive imitation of others; the quest for approval, first from parents and teachers, and later, from social groups and society in general; and what Bushnell called social contagion. This last point refers to the enthusiasm and emotion that influence the character by giving unexamined direction and purpose to people's actions.

These patterns of social influence, Bushnell believed, were integral to the "organic unity" of the family, church, community, or nation. He protested against the prevailing individualism that had "erected the individual mind into a tribunal of judgment within itself," "asserted free will as the ground of all proper responsibility," and held to "theories of religion" that looked upon people as "distinct units" incapable of communicating with one another. In a homely illustration, he described this social condition as one in which individuals "only seem to lie as seeds piled together, without any terms of connection save the accident of proximity." Over against this individualistic pattern, Bushnell claimed the necessary interdependence of state, church, and family as the "three great forms of organic existence" appointed by God.[28]

The commitment to influence lent itself easily to an educational strategy for developing public meanings. The educational agencies of the community already embodied the task of shaping the values and commitments of a future generation. They were manageable in size. The potential for influence might seem more plausible in the context of family, classroom, or congregation than in the forums of law, government, commerce, or even theological debate. The agents of influence—parents, teachers, pastors—could be easily identified and, with effective organization, easily reached. And the focus on influence reinforced the age's fascination with morality more than ideas, with conduct more than motive, with feeling more than intellect, and with children more than with adults.

In summary, Bushnell's view of education focused on the public. The church fulfilled a distinctive role in a strategy that encompassed school, church, and family, and was reinforced by a host of other voluntary agencies, each with a distinctive but interdependent function. The church's task centered on maintaining the presence of religion as a formative influence upon the character of public life. It enlivened the educational work of the school and sustained the moral and religious influence of the family. It reminded the nation of its destiny rooted in the faith of its Puritan ancestors. Hence it played a direct and active role in the education of the public.

## Domestication of Church Education

The general ideological perspective articulated by Bushnell and others in the middle of the nineteenth century continued to dominate the imaginations of the Christian educators who followed them. The editor of the deliberations of the National Education Assembly in 1881, J. C. Hartzell, closed the sessions with prayer, requesting that "Christian patriots may rule our land and that Christian thought may permeate and direct every phase of education in this nation."[29] Speaker after speaker at that conference extolled the necessary interdependence of education and Christianity in shaping the moral character and destiny of the nation. Those speakers did not address themselves to the education of the church. Indeed, the Sunday school associations were not even represented, and the various speakers did not consider the Sunday school's possible contribution to the pressing educational needs of the nation. They assumed that Christians, working through the schools of the public, could influence the national character. For them, the school had become a primary strategy for developing the national paideia; and the church, through those Christian men and women who took public education seriously, influenced the schools. In fact, this view is not far from Bushnell's own assessment of the task of the school in the community.

During the same year another large group of Christian educators gathered for the Third International Sunday School Convention in Toronto. Leaders in this group included Henry Clay Trumbull, who had been elected chairman of its executive committee in 1871; John H. Vincent, Sunday school leader and founder of Chautauqua; and B. F. Jacobs, the convention's new executive secretary. As advocates of the

Sunday school, these men, also, believed that the church contributed to the formation of public meanings and character. In other words they shared a common ideological perspective with their colleagues who were promoting Christian education of the public through the schools. At the same time, their attention to educational strategies increasingly centered upon the Sunday school. They assumed that the church, through the Sunday school, would contribute to the national paideia by making Christians out of the unchurched. In Trumbull's words, "The Sunday-school . . . represents God's chosen agency . . . for the evangelizing and for the instruction of those whom his Church is set to reach and to rear."[30] Vincent's rhetorical power is evident in a similar claim. He described the Sunday school as the preparatory school of the church. Its attention, however, was not to be only on those who grew up in the church. It was to look "beyond the limits of the church, beyond the homes of believers, beyond the bounds of Christian civilization," to those

neglected multitudes to whom the very alphabet of religion is an unknown thing, and the unfamiliar phrases of Christian faith a strange tongue. Children, neglected by parents, pastors, and godly neighbors, are growing up in absolute ignorance. . . . Little careless feet patter about on the steps of stately cathedral, not knowing, save in senseless profanity, the name of the God to whom it is dedicated. Heathen crowds in the centers of Christian civilization! To them come Christian teachers, like Raikes of Gloucester. Opportunity opens, and the Bible teacher enters.[31]

In that role the Bible teacher and the Sunday school cooperated with the family and the pulpit in the task Trumbull saw in the Apostle Paul's Letter to the Ephesians—building up the congregation as "the body of Christ."[32] Vincent, with his colleague Lewis Miller, transformed the Sunday school teacher-training institute they had founded at Chautauqua into a complex of annual meetings, lecture circuits, and literary societies, to embody their larger interest in public issues. But Vincent joined Trumbull in identifying the Sunday school with the church, expecting it to live by and for the church and to train its members to be personally faithful "to the authority, the services, and the enterprises" of the church and its "Divine Head."[33]

The domestication of church education in the formation of the public had begun. Trumbull, Vincent, and other Sunday school leaders increasingly looked upon the Sunday school as the agency of the church's education. The focus on the church intensified as they developed uniform resources, systematized approaches to teacher training, and created bureaucratic structures for Sunday school organization. Their efforts concentrated the energies of Sunday school leaders on evangelization and the nurture of people into the life of the church.

In this shift, Bushnell's vision of the church's public role had been lost. Trumbull and his Sunday school colleagues located Bushnell's views of influence in the church rather than in society, thereby limiting loyalty to a congregation or a denomination and reinforcing the already popular notion of a comprehensive inclusivity to theological simplicity. They appropriated his language on influence to promote teaching and administrative techniques as a means for shaping the behavior and attitudes of children and youth. Perhaps the continuing consequences of this domestication may be seen in the contemporary resistance among many Protestant Christians against engaging in any kind of corporate critique of social or political practice. By limiting church education to the Sunday school, and the Sunday school to evangelization and training in Christian beliefs and morals, the historic emphasis on the separation of church and state has, for many, come to mean the separation of religion and politics. That view is a far cry from Bushnell's belief that his religious responsibilities required him and the church to address directly the political and moral issues facing the community and nation.

Even the language of domesticity permeated the Sunday school descriptions of the church's educational task. Love and influence became inseparable duties of Sunday school teachers. They were to create a homelike atmosphere in the classroom. They were to teach as much by the quality of their own presence as by their comprehension of any lesson. Guides for teachers, for example, often included statements similar to one made by Edward Leigh Pell, who described a certain successful Sunday school teacher as "a holy woman who has been instrumental in the development of more boys into Christian men than any dozen trained teachers I know, and she does not know pedagogy from a potato."[34] Although Sunday school leaders did emphasize the importance of teacher training and worked incessantly at the task of developing curriculum resources, nurturing took precedence over both teaching competence and the content of the faith. It was believed that the personal influence of a teacher could transform the traditional transmissive activities of memorization and recitation into occasions for leading a young person to Christ. Nurture had become integral to evangelizing the public into the life of the church.

The domestication of church education, in other words, may be seen in the delegation of the church's educational responsibilities to the Sunday school, to the limitation of the Sunday school's goals to education in the church, and to the dominance of nurture and influence in the educational process. In contrast to the Puritan view of the church as the foundation of the public and Bushnell's view of the interdependence of religion and the state in forming public character and identity, it was the prevailing view of the Sunday school leaders that the church was the most important of all existing voluntary agencies in the moral transformation of the public. The goal of a Christian nation persisted, but the role of the church increasingly turned inward.

Perhaps the shift in Trumbull's involvement in the public arena illustrates the declining influence of church education in the public forum. In the 1850s he played a critical role in the Republican party organization in Connecticut, in public education, and in the Sunday school. He was a popular lecturer on a wide range of social, political, and religious issues. By the 1880s his contacts with public figures had not lessened. He counted among his friends members of Congress, governors, and even the President. His public role, however, had diminished to that of a former military chaplain, making prayers of invocation and benediction in public ceremonies. He no longer acted as an agent of the church in formative public issues. His attention now was focused upon the strengthening of the church in the nation.

## Clues for the Future

Perhaps the domestication of Protestant church education may be traced partially to the inadequacy of the voluntary educational strategy promulgated by Bushnell and his peers. The interdependence of school, church, and family depended upon the stability and continuity that Bushnell envisioned to have been characteristic of the old Puritan village. Elements of this interdependence could be seen later in the expectation of many in some midwestern communities that teachers in the public school would also teach in the Sunday school, thereby providing that link between civic and religious instruction. Its hold on the imagination of Christian education theorists continued well into the twentieth century, as future chapters will illustrate. And it may still be the guiding image for those across the nation who persist in the dream of a Christian educational ecology, with explicit Christian practices in the schools allied with the churches and families in the nurture of children. But for the most part the strategy was doomed from the beginning, because the educational agencies integral to it simply did not have the power to influence people into the kind of community the educational reformers envisioned.

In the first place, the family could not be depended upon as a disciplined and consistent source of positive influence. Unlike schools and individual churches, the families of a community lacked any cohesive or unifying force. Even as Bushnell and a host of women writers were extolling the educational influence of the family, Frederick Packard, the first secretary of the American Sunday School Union, underscored the usefulness of the Sunday school in influencing parents and other relatives of children "to think upon their ways, and turn their feet unto God's testimonies" through the effects of Sunday school instruction upon their children— "peace, industry, and filial obedience."[35] This theme in the Sunday school literature becomes more pronounced with each passing decade. In his Yale Lectures in 1888, Trumbull rather baldly stated that the Sunday school must support the family in its educational task.[36] Although the rhetoric in his writings seeks to convey the complementary nature of Sunday school and family in the nurture of children, he concluded that the strength of family religion relied upon the proportional strength of the church's school. In the process, one of the functions of the Sunday school was to exert its influence on the family. Indeed, for Trumbull, the extent to which families assumed their religious educational responsibilities depended upon the extent to which the Sunday school supported and sustained the family.

Vincent was even more blunt. He declared that the Sunday school must first "cultivate" the home and then "cooperate" with it by creating a homelike atmosphere in the classroom and by clarifying its expectations of parents in the religious education of their children. In a sample letter to be sent to parents, Vincent described the purposes of the Sunday school:

"to make plain . . . the truths taught in the Holy Scriptures" and to lead students "to love and obey the Lord Jesus Christ." He then observed, "It is exceedingly difficult for us to succeed in this without the help of your parental authority and influence."[37] Once a partner in Bushnell's scheme of things, the family had now become the object of the Sunday school's influence.

A similar problem faced the advocates of the common school. Not only were they forced to contend with the vitriolic criticism of certain segments of the population who feared the common school exemplified the state's encroachment upon the educational responsibilities of local communities; they also had to come to terms with the fact that many parents, especially among the immigrants and poor, did not send their children to school at all. The expectation on the part of the educational reformers that the community would comprehensively support the common schools simply did not often prove to be true. As agents of the state, the advocates of the school responded to the situation quite differently than did the Sunday school leaders. They began to work toward the compulsory attendance of children. Further encroachment on traditional family responsibilities eventually led to extensive course offerings in twentieth-century schools—from cooking to driver education to sex education—programs that would fill the leisure time of students and rules that would structure their social behavior, if not their values, according to the dominant community codes. This shift of responsibility for education during the past hundred years—from parents to school personnel, who feel that parents are often intrusions in their efforts to educate children—may illustrate the extent to which Bushnell's vision of the interdependence of school and family simply does not exist.

Perhaps another reason for the collapse of the strategy may be located in the lack, from the outset, of any viable cohering force—a problem that continued well into the twentieth century. Bushnell assumed that the interdependence of school, church, and family would be sustained by the community. Perhaps his own memories of the interlocking network of relationships in the village of Litchfield County in Connecticut dominated his imagination. But his vision of an educational ecology was grounded in voluntary assumptions that must be consistently renewed if they are to be maintained. The social glue of informal socialization patterns, for example, lacks the external objectivity of legal structures in providing continuity in a time of rapid social change. Similarly, the mid-century Protestant churches' almost immediate acceptance of the Sunday school as their primary educational agency, and the somewhat more reticent acceptance of the common school as the community's primary educational agency, meant that the traditional expectations regarding the relationship of church and community evident in Bushnell's writings were no longer useful. The attention of both common school and Sunday school leaders was increasingly diverted to symbols of permanence (buildings and organizational charts), to patterns of centralized control, and to negotiation of internal conflicts and differences.[38] In this case, both continued to employ rhetoric regarding the contribution of their agencies for the building up of a patriotic and Christian nation, but their actions increasingly concentrated upon internal matters.

Perhaps even more significant, such traditional expectations of education as the transmission of cultural values and the incorporation of a new generation into the life of the community took a backseat to the pressing need to assimilate those whom these Christian educators feared might disrupt the social, political, economic, and spiritual order of the nation. The potential in the civilizing influence of the schools and the Sunday schools quickly preempted other concerns. It is fascinating to observe that in spite of his commitment to the importance of the intellectual life, Bushnell's own statements about the common schools emphasized the ameliorating effect of the school environment on the diverse populations of the community; these only reflected the rhetoric that helped to sway many leading citizens in the cities of the region to support the schools. Trumbull would similarly claim that one of the contributions of the Sunday school existed in its checking the "flood of godless immigration" which threatened to absorb "all vestiges of Christianity as a vitalizing force in the newer communities of our extending border population."[39] Trumbull's own experience undoubtedly influenced his perceptions. As a young man, he had witnessed the "comprehensive" potential of the Sunday school while teaching at the Morgan Street school in Hartford. He noted that when the enrollment reached almost two hundred, the school included "about twenty Jews, seventy-five Roman Catholics, forty blacks, and others of some nine different nationalities."[40] He assumed, however, that this school was preparing its members to leave the rough society in which they lived to be assimilated into the ethos of a rising Christian middle class. As a social principle, comprehensiveness simply did not address the radical character of the diverse economic or racial distinctions of the United States populace. Catholics had been present long enough and in sufficient numbers to begin to claim a place for themselves in the public economy, and the result was more than disconcerting to the advocates of a common school-church-family ecology for the education of the public. For Jews, that step was still to come. For the factory worker it would not occur until the labor unions provided a unifying voice. For blacks the process would take still longer. And for the Native American the articulation of that claim has only recently begun to be heard. The vision of a comprehensive society was still too Protestant in its emphasis upon the interdependence of a nation's voluntary organisms, too restrictive in its lack of real attention to the place of nonwhite populations in its vision of the national destiny, and too middle class.

By the latter part of the nineteenth century the themes in Bushnell's vision of a "Christian America" continued to dominate the imagination of educators in the church. His language was not necessarily used, but the issue of national destiny to be found in the character of a people distinguished by their faith in God persisted. The nation's mission to the world was located in its commitment to righteousness. This revised vision celebrated the nation's heritage but also welcomed the challenges of expansion, industrialization, and cultural diversification.

Today we may recognize the chauvinism and parochialism in that vision, but for decades it has been central to the sense of nationhood for countless millions. We may also begin to comprehend some of the reasons for the continuing restiveness of the populace as a result of its commitment to education as the primary means for developing public consciousness, identity, and purpose. Our rhetoric continues to value the educational contributions of school, church, and family. At the same time, these same agencies are continually criticized for their inability to fulfill our expectations. We continue to believe that the church has a formative role to play in the public. At the same time, we have not yet come to terms with the domestication of the church's contribution to public life.

## Notes

1. Horace Bushnell, "American Politics," *The American National Preacher* 14/12 (December 1840):191.
2. Horace Bushnell, *Politics Under the Law of God* (Hartford: E. Hunt, 1844), p. 6.
3. David Tyack, "The Kingdom of God and the Common School," *Harvard Educational Review* 36 (Fall 1966):448. The story to this point has centered primarily upon those white evangelical churches whose membership provided both the economic and political leadership of the nation and whose status depended significantly upon stability in all

sectors of the nation's life. The views of the circuit riders, the southern clergy ministering to slaveholders, the millennialists, the priests of both the rapidly growing Roman Catholic immigrant churches and the Spanish settlements of the Southwest, as well as those Christian leaders in black and Native American communities, have yet to be explored in any depth.

4. J. C. Hartzell, ed., *Christian Educators in Council: Sixty Addresses by American Educators with Historic Notes upon the National Education Assembly* (New York: Phillips & Hunt, 1884).

5. Cf. R.W.B. Lewis, *The American Adam: Innocence, Tragedy, and Tradition in the Nineteenth Century* (Chicago: University of Chicago Press, 1955); William A. Clebsch, *From Sacred to Profane America: The Role of Religion in America* (New York: Harper & Row, 1968); Ann Douglas, *The Feminization of American Culture* (New York: Avon Books, 1977); Martin E. Marty, *Righteous Empire: The Protestant Experience in America* (New York: Dial Press, 1970).

6. Bushnell was often quoted by progressive religious educators, especially to identify someone in the mid-century who discussed religious education as a nurturing process. No one undertook a serious study of his views on religious education, however, until Alexander J. W. Myers wrote *Horace Bushnell and Religious Education* (Boston: Manthorne & Burack, 1937). The lack of attention to Bushnell's thought did not preclude Karl A. Stolz from describing him as "the morning star" of the religious education movement ("Historical Development of Religious Education in America," in *Studies in Religious Education,* ed. Philip Henry Lotz and L. W. Crawford [Nashville: Cokesbury Press, 1931], p. 31). Harrison Elliott (*Can Religious Education Be Christian?* [New York: Macmillan Co., 1940], p. 33) would later observe the irony in his colleagues' description of Bushnell as the "father" of religious education when they concentrated their attention upon the theological rather than the educational issues in his writing.

7. H. Clay Trumbull, *Teaching and Teachers; or The Sunday-school Teacher's Teaching Work and the Other Work of the Sunday-school Teacher* (Philadelphia: John D. Wattles, 1885), p. 265; *My Four Religious Teachers* (Philadelphia: *The Sunday School Times,* 1903), pp. 9-10, 73-74.

8. Clebsch, *From Sacred to Profane,* p. 193.

9. Sidney E. Mead, *The Nation with the Soul of a Church* (New York: Harper & Row, 1975), p. 64; "Extracts of a Report of Dr. Bushnell's Fast Day Discourse," *New England Religious Herald* (April 29, 1848).

10. Henry Clay Trumbull, *Shoes and Rations for a Long March; or Needs and Supplies in Every-day Life* (New York: Charles Scribner's Sons, 1903), p. 254.

11. William C. Clebsch, "Baptism of Blood: A Study of Christian Contributions to the Interpretation of the Civil War in American History" (Ph.D. diss., Union Theological Seminary, 1957), p. 75.

12. Marty, *Righteous Empire,* p. 87.

13. Horace Bushnell, "Christianity and Common Schools," *Connecticut Common School Journal* 2 (January 15, 1841):103.
14. Horace Bushnell, letter to the editor, *Christian Freeman* 2/50 (December 12, 1844):2.
15. Bushnell, "Christianity and Common Schools," p. 102.
16. Horace Bushnell, *Building Eras in Religion* (New York: Charles Scribner's Sons, 1881), "Common Schools," p. 76.
17. *The Republic and the Schools: Horace Mann on the Education of Free Men,* ed. Lawrence A. Cremin (New York: Bureau of Publications, Teachers College, Columbia University, 1957), pp. 32-33.
18. Bushnell, *Building Eras,* p. 97.
19. Horace Bushnell, *Christian Nurture* (New Haven: Yale University Press, 1888 [1960]), p. 184.
20. Ibid., p. 89.
21. Horace Bushnell, *Work and Play* (London: Richard D. Dickinson, 1888), "The Doctrine of Loyalty Working Itself Out in America," pp. 267, 263.
22. James M. Gustafson, "The Voluntary Church: A Moral Appraisal," in *Voluntary Associations: A Study of Groups in Free Societies,* ed. D. B. Robertson (Richmond: John Knox Press, 1966), p. 315. Bushnell's theory of comprehensiveness did not encompass all peoples. He expected non-Christians to accommodate their aspirations in the public life to that of the Christian majority. In spite of his strong antislavery commitments, he never envisioned a place for the black population in the national economy. Similarly, he decried the Trail of Tears across the Southeast to Oklahoma, but he apparently did not explore the possibility of Native American participation in public life. For a more detailed discussion of his views on slavery and black presence in the nation, see Douglas, *Feminization of American Culture,* p. 38ff., and Clebsch, "Baptism of Blood."
23. Horace Bushnell, *God in Christ* (Hartford: Brown & Parsons, 1849), p. 80.
24. Bushnell, *Building Eras,* pp. 103-5.
25. Bushnell, *Christian Nurture,* p. 85.
26. Trumbull, *Teaching and Teachers,* p. 265.
27. Douglas, *Feminization of American Culture,* p. 8.
28. Bushnell, *Christian Nurture,* p. 75.
29. Hartzell, *Sixty Addresses,* p. 232.
30. Henry Clay Trumbull, *The Sunday-School: Its Origin, Mission, Methods, and Auxiliaries* (Philadelphia: John D. Wattles, 1888), p. VI.
31. John H. Vincent, *The Modern Sunday School* (New York: Eaton & Mains, 1887 [1900]), p. 13.
32. Trumbull, *Teaching and Teachers,* p. 212.
33. Vincent, *Modern Sunday School,* p. 22.
34. Edward Leigh Pell, *Secrets of Sunday School Teaching* (New York: Fleming H. Revell, 1912), p. 13.

35. Frederick A. Packard, *Teacher Taught* (Philadelphia: American Sunday School Union, 1839), p. 35.
36. Trumbull, *The Sunday-School,* pp. 155-56.
37. Vincent, *Modern Sunday School,* pp. 22-29.
38. Seymour B. Sarason, *The Creation of Settings and the Future Societies* (San Francisco: Jossey-Bass, 1972), describes this rather common process in the institutionalization of the dreams of people. His analysis provides useful clues to the tempering of the vision of the Sunday school advocates, the socialization of these same advocates in the political struggles over the control and direction of the Sunday school, and the increasingly self-serving focus of the Sunday school in the larger community.
39. Trumbull, *Teaching and Teachers,* p. 122.
40. Philip E. Howard, *The Life Story of Henry Clay Trumbull: Missionary, Army Chaplain, Editor and Author* (Philadelphia: *The Sunday School Times,* 1905), p. 111.

# American and Catholic: The Education of a People Within the Public

IN 1785 at Versailles, Pope Pius VI's nuncio met with Benjamin Franklin to seek advice from Congress on the appointment of a leader for the freshly emancipated Catholics in the newly formed United States. The response from Congress read: "The subject of his [the nuncio's] application to Doctor Franklin, being purely spiritual, it is without the jurisdiction and powers of Congress who have no authority to permit or refuse it."[1]

This historic incident illustrates the radical adjustment necessary for Catholicism as a church in the United States. Since the religious emancipation of Catholics in this country occurred only after the new nation's separation from a religiously intolerant England, the nineteenth century is foundational in the establishment of this church's people as part of the national public.

Historically, the Christian religion has defined itself in its dialogue with society. Each culture has played a role in this process: the Jewish, the Greek, the Roman, the European, the North American, the Latin American, the Asian, and so on. In each society, Christianity has assumed particular characteristics which have become a permanent part of its universal expression in a continual evolution. Thus it has been the relationship with a nonsectarian state that has produced the peculiar spirit of Catholicism in the United States.

This relationship raised four significant issues for the Catholic Church. First, since the federal constitution prohibited the establishment of any church as *the* religion of the land, the church needed to rework its self-concept. Although the religious pluralism in the Constitution served to protect the minority status of Catholics, it caused theological problems with the Catholic belief in *one* true church. Therefore the first problem was that of religious tolerance.

Second, the nation's republicanism embodied not merely a break with the church as a partner in government, but a break also with the authoritarian form of rule employed by the European states. The Catholic Church, in coexisting with European civil government, had fashioned its own polity according to that authoritarian form. However, this new form of government spawned an antithesis to that authoritarianism—voluntarism—in which the Catholic polity of hierarchial relation to Rome had to struggle to survive. For example, the church fought the "lay-trusteeism" movement (copied from congregationalism) as its first heresy in the United States. The second problem was that of church polity.

Third, in this land whose government would not enter into concordat with the church, this problem arose: How could the church affect the moral behavior of its people in regard to birth, marriage, divorce, death, burial, and so on? It was forced to sort out the religious from the civic in human life, a task Judaism had faced under Roman occupation ("Render unto Caesar . . ."). However, after the time of Constantine the Catholic Church had not faced this problem again until its experience in the United States. The third problem was that of church-state separation.

Fourth, in regard to the formation of the young, the church was confronted with the rise and development of universal schooling and the prospect of giving up its influence in formal education to the state. It also envisioned schooling as a possible way to carry out its aim of fashioning a people, and, in a time and place that would be concerned with schooling as a major agency of formation, the Catholic Church would have great difficulty in separating religion from education. The fourth problem was with the relation of religion to education.

Here, then, are the four crucial issues the Catholic Church faced in constructing its identity in the nineteenth century. It was in struggling with these problems that the Catholic people engaged their relationships to the public. In this engagement they both strategized for the survival of their own identity and participated in the construction of the "American" paideia.

## Social Environment

The development of the ethos for the church's educational task is a product of its struggle with these four issues and took place in the context of social developments in the larger environment of the national culture. The very goals, as well as the means, were formulated in conjunction with and/or in contrast to the major events of the times.

Four factors in the social environment of the nineteenth century were influential in the formation of Catholic values and as the means to achieve them: immigration, nativist reaction, secularization, and educational reform.

The story of immigration can be told from its population statistics. When Roman Catholics began their life in the United States at the time of the Revolution, their numbers accounted for only 1.1 percent of the population (35,000 of the 3,172,000 people who were considered citizens in 1790). From 1790 until 1880, most immigrants were Irish and German Europeans, and the Roman Catholic share of the population grew to 14.4 percent. From 1830 until 1880, 30 percent of the population increase was due to immigration; and 40 percent of that immigration was Roman Catholic. Furthermore, the number of foreign born in major cities was staggering. For example, in 1860, 49 percent of New York City's population and 30 percent of Philadelphia's was foreign born. Saint Louis had a foreign-born population of 60 percent; Chicago, 50 percent. By 1850, almost 60 percent of all Roman Catholics were foreign born. "Foreign" and "Catholic" became synonymous; to react to the one was to react to the other.

*Nativism* is the term historians use to describe the reaction of those born in this country to people who immigrated here. If one thinks of how, in biological life, the host body fights to reject foreign matter that enters it, one can conceptualize the relationship of "native" Protestants to "foreign" Roman Catholics in the nineteenth century.

A look at any one of the three million copies of the *New England Primer* from 1700 to 1850 reveals the residual of Old-World anti-Catholicism that pervaded the colonies before the number of Catholics was significant. When that number did begin to increase, so did the literary attacks. Samuel B. F. Morris' *Foreign Conspiracy* in the 1830s predicted a papal plot to take over the Midwest. The *Awful Disclosures of Maria Monk* provided Protestants with malicious images of Catholic priests and nuns. And Thomas Nast's political cartoons, in the minds of Protestants, linked the Roman Catholic hierarchy with tyranny. In the 1840s this nativism took the form of civil riot. Catholic churches were closed in Philadelphia, convents were burned in Boston, and in the streets of New York, Catholics armed for defense. In the 1850s this nativism developed into political and economic discrimination. Catholics, in reaction, retreated to island communities (generally the cities) in the face of this most effective resistance. They set up social and religious structures that kept their private life separate from public life; in this way they were "in" but not "of" the public.

With the nineteenth century came a decline of religion in

the public life of society. The democratic faith that had developed in the eighteenth century was transformed from a theistic to a scientific texture, and religion was challenged as the basis for knowing truth. Laws disestablished churches in the individual states, and the union of religion and education, evident in the earlier nineteenth-century efforts of Horace Mann, dissolved under the leadership of William Torry Harris, United States Commissioner of Education, at the end of that century. While this rise of secularization was mourned by most church people, Catholics refused to accept a community life in which the religious and the secular were separate. And on their islands, they did not need to accept it.

The reform of education was the fourth element to affect Catholics in the nineteenth-century social environment. The purpose of the reform was to create a new institution in society—the public school—with the formation of a common life as its goal. A common culture was to be shaped and transmitted, not by family and tribe, but by this new development of modern society, which proposed to educate and form the very heart and soul of the nation. This instrument of cultural formation, the common school, became compulsory—that is, conducted and enforced by the state. Catholics, however, refused to hand their young over to any institution that either embodied Protestantism or separated religion and education. In Catholic eyes, the Protestant way of accommodating public education by establishing the church Sunday school only reinforced the "heretical" concept that religion and education could be separated. Catholics did not believe religion could be separated from education, any more than culture and education could be separated.

## The Two Spirits of Nineteenth-Century Catholicism

In light of this background, two distinct spirits become apparent in the Catholic identity formation, representing the

Roman Catholic relationship to the public culture: one, the accommodationist, urged inclusivity; the other, the isolationist, insisted upon separation. These two spirits struggled both with each other and with the larger social environment in determining the forms of the church's ministries, especially that of education.

## The Accommodationist Position

The first of the two spirits, the spirit of accommodation, arose from a positive experience of the United States as liberating, with freedom to exercise social, economic, political, and religious choice. This position's intellectual reflections can be found in the writings of Father Isaac T. Hecker (1819–1888).[2]

One of Hecker's key beliefs was that the church had entered an age in which the focal point of its mission (the salvation of souls) should cease to be its own authority and should become the liberty and dignity of the individual. This idea represented an innovation for Catholicism. It broke with the tradition that had held sway since the Council of Trent when the church had reacted to the revolt of the "would-be" Reformers. That three-hundred-year Counter Reformation emphasized authority, the absolute authority of the church in matters of faith and morals.[3]

Father Hecker had come to the Catholic Church as an adult. A follower of the transcendental movement, he was a "native American," proud of his country's growth and progress. The religious society he founded (the Missionary Society of St. Paul—the Paulists) was aimed at promoting an emphasis on liberty in the religious sphere.

Hecker believed that liberty was God's grace, an inestimable gift that meant freedom from slavery, including the slavery of authority. He held an evolutionary view of the mission of the church—that it was moving into a new and fresh phase of life, that the essence of Roman Catholicism was not authority, but "the elevation of rational creatures, by the power of the Holy Spirit, to a union with God above that which they enjoy by their birth." The normal orbit of the church is a course "characterized by spontaneity, expansion, individual initiative, and energetic action." For Hecker, "Christianity is truth, and invites men to exercise their faculties in search after truth and emancipate themselves from all servitude. 'You shall know the truth,' so runs the Master's promise, 'and the truth shall make you free.' This is Catholicity."[4]

Walter Ong, in a literary and theological reflection on the life and thought of Father Hecker, has described him as "particularly sensitive to America as a symbol, and to certain symbols by which Americans lived—liberty, the idea of hard work, expansiveness and 'optimism,' resourcefulness—and he was burning with a desire to infuse these ideals with a Catholic spirit."[5] Thus Isaac Hecker, born in this country, bred in its "native" religion, and entering the Catholic church as an adult, desired to effect a synthesis between nature as he experienced it in the United States—free, fresh, expansive and optimistic—and grace as he experienced it in the Catholic religion—spontaneous, expansive, energetic. For him, as for Paul, the apostle he idealized, the essence of Christianity was freedom.

Because of the centrality of freedom in the spirit of Hecker, it has often been referred to as the liberal spirit. Such a label, however, can be and has been misleading when the frame of reference for that word is *Europe*. Hecker's liberalism was not a "European import," a Jacobean totalitarian liberalism, but the liberalism of a new civilization.[6] The post-Civil War secular culture was far less hostile to the church than was the situation in Europe. The experience out of which the accommodationist spirit of Catholicism arose was the positive and optimistic one of Catholic bishops such as John Carroll, John England, the Spaldings, James Roosevelt Bailey,

Thomas Grace, John Ireland, and those of a similar mind: This country was a land in which one could exercise social, political, economic, and religious initiative; a land in which one was invited—not coerced—to join a political, social, economic, or religious persuasion; a land in which a social, political, economic, or religious institution stood or fell on its own intrinsic goodness, not by virtue of its enforcement by the state.

Because religion was a "free enterprise," the "image" of the church was of the utmost concern. For the accommodationists, this meant that the church must be "sold" to their fellow citizens, thus accepting the voluntary spirit of life. It was this concern that helped move the church to become an agency for "Americanization" of the immigrants. In order to make the church attractive and to influence public life, accommodationists believed immigrant Catholics should forsake saloons and poverty, give up their European culture, and attempt entry into the mainstream. Some accommodationists went so far as to urge that Catholic children attend public schools. Those who were not so radical desired to make the Catholic schools at least as "American" as possible, and they championed compulsory education. Protestant United States responded favorably to these accommodationist views. Much of the thought and action of the accommodationists was shaped by Protestant fears that the Catholic Church's claim of supremacy over morals extended also to politics. Hecker exploded the false myth that democracy sprang from Protestantism while Roman Catholicism was, by nature and in essence, authoritarian, and thus inimical to liberty.

Nevertheless, the accommodationist spirit had inherent liabilities. It suffered from too much action and not enough reflection. Its emphasis on initiative and enterprise often failed to explore the theoretical, especially the theological implications of its position. In practice, it produced too heady a spirit in those who tied it to the nation's military, economic, and political expansionism and tried to export it to the Catholic Church in Europe, where its more distant relative, Jacobean totalitarian liberalism, was being accorded a very negative reception.

## The Isolationist Position

The other spirit of Catholicism in the United States grew out of an experience of persecution, bigotry, and oppression. The roots of isolationism went back to pre-Revolutionary times and the Puritan intolerance of the "popish" religion, when the colonies were a British possession, subject to that empire's penal laws. The periods of post-Revolutionary history most vivid to the isolationists were those when churches and convents were burned in civil riots, times when Catholic children were corporally punished for refusing to read the King James Version of the Bible or participate in a Protestant form of worship in the common school. They took personally the slanderous bigotry of "know-nothingism" and the Ku Klux Klan, as well as the social, economic, and political discrimination that arose as a Protestant reaction to heavy Catholic immigration. These Catholics saw the same totalitarianism in both European and United States liberalism, and they embraced its Roman condemnation as their creed.

The antimodernist reflections of Pius IX served as the theory for their practice. He envisioned his task to be a clear and explicit denunciation of the very foundations of liberalism—the self-enabled enlightenment of the human being. In declarations, all issued on December 8 (1854, 1864, and 1869 respectively), the pope made a categorical denial of liberalism.

In *Ineffabilis Deus,* defining the doctrine of the Immaculate Conception (declaring Mary's freedom from the legacy of original sin), the pope reiterated and underscored the church's insistence on the reality of the supernatural and the validity of religious mysteries. He reaffirmed the fact of the human legacy of sin and struck directly at the foundation of liberal faith, attacking the idea of immutable, unboundless progress and the innate goodness of the human being. Mary, in other words, was the exception that proved the rule.

The *Syllabus of Errors* consisted of eighty propositions concerning the supernatural principles of faith, the existence of God and Providence, the constitution of the church, modern errors due to Protestant infiltration (such as indifferentism and rationalism), and errors in regard to the modern state (such as liberalism, socialism, and progress). The syllabus denounced the breaking down of social organizations into closed compartments, which prohibited the permeation of the whole of society with a single, transcendent moral purpose. It assailed the secularization of politics.

Finally, with the pronouncement of papal infallibility in the First Council of the Vatican, the pope reaffirmed the historic faith in the supernatural origin of man and woman and reasserted the supranational character of the church.

The isolationists believed it impossible to harmonize Catholicism and "Americanism." Their constant attempts to secure public funds for the Catholic schools attested to their refusal to comprehend the nation's position regarding the separation of church and state. According to this position, as expressed in education, the purpose of the school was to create a national public, and the people as a whole were to determine the policy of publicly supported institutions. The very establishment of Catholic schools was a declaration by the isolationists that the Roman Catholic way of life was different from that of other people in the United States.

The isolationists were most concerned about the areas of moral behavior, encompassing such issues as birth and marriage. The state considered many of these moral issues to be under the control of democratic government. The rise of democracy scuttled the notion that the church alone had the right to teach. The church of these isolationists, however, had declared itself the authoritative teacher in these areas. The clash was not only over who was supreme, but also over the manner in which decisions in these matters of morals were reached—whether by authoritative or by democratic rule.[7]

It should be pointed out that several of the isolationists were opposed to the definition of papal infallibility. This resistance was not, however, due as much to theological differences as to a shell-shocked group's fear of repercussions from this promulgation, in terms of abuse they might endure from nativists.

The isolationists were not concerned with gaining converts to Catholicism, but with providing a safe base for those already in the church. The rise of industrialization and heavy immigration produced such rapid social change and growth in the church's population that the isolationists saw the conservation of the faith as their all-consuming task.

In reflecting on this spirit it is clear that the isolationist mentality, as enacted in the United States, eventuated in the very error condemned by the pope's syllabus—the separation of faith and moral life. The Catholic citizen's life was thus compartmentalized into domestic and public realms. Social matters such as marriage, birth, and education were confined to the island where the church would rule, but the Catholic's public-business life took place off the island, apart from the church.

## The Educational Interaction of Church and Public

The manifestation of these two spirits is apparent in the educational leadership of the Catholic Church in its foundational period. Two key figures dominated Catholic education at the end of the nineteenth century: John Ireland, the accommodationist; and Bernard McQuaid, the isolationist. It is during the life and times of these two bishops that major policy decisions were made as to the focus and meaning of the

Catholic Church's mission and ministry in education for the major portion of the twentieth century.

## Accommodationists:
### The Church and the Public in Education

The list of those who provided leadership in the nineteenth century in the marriage between Catholicism and the emerging culture begins with John Carroll (1735–1815). He and his prominant Maryland family had a significant place in the founding of the United States. He also served as a delegate to the French Catholic leaders of Canada in an unsuccessful attempt to rally Canada to the cause of the Revolution. When installed as the church's first bishop, he declared his position on the way the church should relate to the public: "It is no longer enough for me to be inoffensive in my conduct and regular in my manners. God now imposes a severer duty upon me."[8] Among his first actions was the establishment of Catholic centers of learning: Georgetown (1791), St. Mary's Seminary (1791), and St. Mary's College (1799).

Next is Bishop John England of Charleston (1786–1842), who can be noted for two accommodationist contributions. In the 1820s he founded *The U.S. Catholic Missallany*. This first Catholic periodical in the United States set a high tone of literary discourse in speaking to Protestants about Catholicism's compatibility with the way of life in the United States.

Second, he, more than any of the nation's Catholic leaders to this day, fashioned a form of church governance for his diocese that clearly separated lay and clerical influence over fiscal and spiritual matters. He attempted to extend this more "American" church polity to the universal Catholic Church by his call for collegiality of bishops with the pope.[9]

The most powerful and prominent leader to attempt to accommodate the Catholic Church's educational ministries to United States culture was John Ireland (1838–1918), the

Archbishop of Saint Paul. In his 1890 speech to the National Education Association (NEA), Ireland praised the state schools and their right to educate, making such forthright declarations as "I would have all schools for the children of the people to be state schools," and "The free school of America! Withered be the hand raised in sign of its destruction."[10] He enunciated two principles of education: (1) Religion was a vital part of a child's school education; and (2) the best way to provide this religious education for all children was in the nation's public schools. In this NEA speech, Ireland made it clear that he approved the method the United States had employed to provide free universal education. He cited the conditions of the modern age, which both demanded more from its citizens educationally and permitted less time for parents to provide this themselves. In his opinion, the state's method, in its attempt to be nonsectarian, had, in fact, become secular by indirectly teaching a divorce of religion from education. Ireland maintained that Catholics and some groups of Protestants conducted parish schools solely to counteract this separation. "The teaching of religion," he stated, "is not a function of the state; but the State should, for the sake of its people, and for its own sake, permit and facilitate the teaching of religion by the Church."[11]

Ireland believed that nonsectarianism differed from secularism, but that in nonsectarian schools, with the absence of "positive" religion, the religion of secularism had emerged by default. Since he felt that morals are required to maintain a good society and that morals derive their power and vitality only from the principles of positive religion, Ireland concluded that the nation's citizens required positive religious training. This, he said, was precluded by a school system based on nonsectarian principles.

He called for a strategy of public schooling that would reflect the people's concern for religion and schooling but would also respect a pluralism of religious orientations, a way for church to relate to state, for religion to relate to culture in an age of democracy.

Ireland's dream was built upon a positive and optimistic view of the position of the church in the modern world. He believed that the world had moved into a new age—one in which the individual was rising to greater heights of reason and liberty, to perfect enjoyment of his or her natural rights.

> We are advancing towards one of those great epochs of history, in which mighty changes will be wrought. The world is in throes; a new age is to be born. . . . All things which may be changed will be changed, and nothing will be tomorrow as it was yesterday, save that which emanates directly from God, or which the Eternal Power decrees to be permanent.[12]

In this new age, Ireland considered the ideal relationship of church and society to be analogous to the relationship of body and soul, nature and grace—a separation that respects mutual freedom of operation, but a union of cooperation and development.

To the bishop, the United States represented the best political institution for this new age. He declared that his Catholic heart and his "American" heart were one, that there was no problem of compatibility between church and country. In lecturing on the "Mission of Catholics in America," Ireland recalled Orestes Brownson's words:

> "Never since her going forth from that upper room in Jerusalem, has the Church found a national character so well fitted to give her civilization its highest and noblest expression." The supernatural rests upon the natural which it purifies and enables, adding to it supernatural gifts of grace and glory. When the natural is most carefully cultivated, there will be found the best results from the union of nature and grace. The American people made Catholic, nowhere shall we find a higher order of Christian civilization than in America.[13]

In his speeches that encouraged the blending of church and country, Ireland attacked those who supported a retreat of the church from society, claiming that such a position is contrary to Catholic tradition.

Since he viewed the world as the place where salvation is effected, Ireland called on Catholics to bring the church's solutions to the ever continuing problem of people's worldly existence. He urged Catholics to stop their denunciations of the age and show themselves as true friends of progressivism. To carry out their mission to the public, they must become models of "Americanism" and personal righteousness. Ireland refused to take nativist bigotry seriously. Instead, he proposed peaceful and dignified answers to those attacks and opposed the forming of organizations to respond to anti-Catholic propaganda. Catholics must not pose as martyrs, attributing all their misfortunes to the persecution of their faith. And it was contrary to their mission to be boastful when one of their own came into prominence. The bishop fought against the formation of a Catholic block in any political party. According to his view of the church's mission, he supported everything that would cultivate human rights: temperance, western migration from the immigrant-city slums, liberal education.

Ireland was determined to reform the ministries of the church to support the tendencies of the natural order. In this description of ideal Catholics, note that the rhetoric is similar to that of Bushnell.

In the fulfillment of their mission the chief need of Catholic laity is leaders—men of *élite*, well-trained in faith and morals, resolute and reliable, model men, who will form after their own character the mass of their fellow-Catholics, and will be the representatives of the Church before the country in all movements making for truth and moral goodness. Model men, assuredly, must they be who are to be the standard bearers of the armies of the Church. They must be second to none in the power and the accomplishments of a superior education. Authority and influence, such as nothing else supplies, issue forth from a rich and well-developed mind. Wherever intelligence is at work, in literature, in scientific inquiry, in the management of large enterprises, in statesmanship, Catholic leaders must occupy distinguished places. In private life they must be stainless and above reproach, distinguished by their sobriety, their pure morals, their probity, in dealing with others—the most honorable of men; in public life they must be the best of citizens, marked by unswerving loyalty to public duty, by generous and unselfish love of country and its institutions—the most faithful, the most ardent of Americans.[14]

## Isolationists: The Church and the Public in Education

Orestes Brownson (1803–1876) is the most focused nineteenth-century thinker on the relationship of education to Catholicism and to United States culture. In 1844 he entered the Catholic Church and exercised his influence as a writer and lecturer until his death. His stance moved from a type of accommodation to isolation. In an 1837 lecture he presented his understanding of education:

Education is something more than is commonly understood by the term. Education is something more than the ability to read and write and cypher, with a smattering of Grammar, Geography and History into the bargain. It is not acquired in schools only, in the few months or the few years our children are in the school-room. It begins with the first impression made on the senses of the infant, and ends only with the last made on those of the man before he sinks into the grave. Its process is ever going on. The conversation, habits and conduct of parents; the spirit, manners and morals of brothers and sisters, of playmates, companions, associates and of the whole society, all contribute to it and aid in determining its character. These influences make up the real education received. Our schools do, and can do but little.[15]

Note how Brownson, who was self-educated, saw education as being composed of several agencies, as does Lawrence

Cremin a century later. Brownson also focused his educational concerns on the church, the family, the press, and adult voluntary societies of all types, as well as literature and lecture programs.

After his conversion Brownson set out to Catholicize the United States. In 1850, however, 60 percent of Catholics were foreign born, and Brownson believed that to carry out the task of Catholicizing, his fellow church members must first be "Americanized." For the rest of his life Brownson struggled with the common-school system and its power to "Americanize" as it became a much more significant agency for character formation than it had been in the 1830s.

In the beginning of this struggle he championed public school attendance for Catholic immigrant children, since "he had no fear that the schools were capable of doing such damage to the faith of Catholic children, for non-Catholics had overstated the potency of schooling."[16] By 1862, however, Brownson began to shift his position on schooling's power in cultural formation and now openly supported Catholic schools as necessary for Catholic children. In so doing, he went on to define a Catholic education—which Catholic schools must supply, and against which their suitability should be judged. That education must hold out for a universal truth in all areas of life. Its goal and the mission of the church were one and the same—to complete the incarnation of the Word in the world. Brownson maintained that for education to be Catholic, it must tend toward the union of the two natures—human and divine—that is, civilization and religion. Synthesis of nature and grace was the aim of Christ, of the church, and of Catholic education.[17]

Catholic education, thought Brownson, prepared people to be part of "the American civilization—the most advanced civilization the world has yet seen[. It] comes nearer to the realization of the Catholic ideal than any which has been heretofore developed and actualized."[18] Brownson hoped that Catholic schools would give up their commitment to Old World education, which he believed would reduce the United States to a stagnant civilization. In later writings he indicated his disappointment with the inability of public schools to carry out the Catholic ideal of education (the "true ideal"), and he supported separate Catholic schools even more strongly.

By the end of his life, Brownson, who in 1862 had praised this country's civilization as the most advanced, was becoming increasingly cynical of the society. Eventually it was the preservation of the faith of Catholic children, rather than the Catholization of society that became his primary concern. Schooling, which he once considered least significant as an agency of education, now became of major importance. Thus when his life ended, he was promoting the crusade for Catholic schools. It can be concluded that due to his disenchantment with United States society, and even his fear of it, Brownson contributed to the domestication of Catholic religious education by making an anti-public school stance characteristic of the "Catholic school mentality."

Brownson, then, was influential in both the accommodationist and the isolationist camp, beginning in the former and ending in the latter.

One of the first Catholic bishops faced with the school question was John Hughes (1797–1864), the Archbishop of New York. The state of New York did not take direct responsibility for educating the masses in the city, but provided money to the philanthropic Public School Society, which was Protestant in orientation. The efforts of this group, however, were inadequate to handle all the city's poor. Hughes believed that his Catholics were being socially deprived by this system of schooling; yet at the same time, he was determined to keep the immigrants tied to himself and to the church. This controversy between the New York Public School Society on the one hand, and Hughes on the other, gives us a picture of the origin of schooling for the majority of Catholics, the masses of the lower classes.

From 1840 until 1842, Hughes fought against the schools of the privately controlled but publicly funded Public School Society because they represented "a chauvinistic, pan-Protestant point of view."[19] Due to his vigorous efforts to seek state funds for schools that would be under his control, the state legislated that the city's schools be nonsectarian and accepted their control. Hughes then assumed responsibility for the education of the Catholic poor, stating, "I think the time has come when it will be necessary to build the schoolhouse first, and the Church afterwards."[20]

The German-heritage bishops were the most united group in the isolationist camp. Their influence was strongest in the Midwest where there were great concentrations of German immigrants: Cincinnati, Saint Louis, Milwaukee, and areas of Wisconsin and Minnesota. Those bishops believed strongly in the power of language to contain the faith and the culture, as expressed in their motto, With the Language Goes the Faith. In the parochial school their children could be taught in the German language; this was illegal in public schools. So concerned were they that they appealed to Rome to establish a German-speaking national hierarchy in this country—one that would exist alongside the English-speaking hierarchy. Between 1830 and 1880, immigration accounted for 57 percent of the Catholic increase in population, and 25 percent of that immigration was German-speaking. Had Rome granted their desire, there would have been a major division in Catholicism in the United States.

The editor of the New York *Freeman's Journal,* James McMaster (1820–1886), a lay convert from Scottish Presbyterianism, played a key role in supporting the isolation of Catholic children from the national culture. In 1872 he stated editorially that church law condemned any system of child training that was not under the supervision of approved

Catholic teachers; that "the time has come to enforce *everywhere,* the general law of the Catholic church, that Catholics must not send their children to any school except Catholic schools."[21] The "law" to which McMaster referred was contained in Pope Pius IX's *Syllabus* and was originally an instruction sent to the Archbishop of Freiburg in Breisgan. The pope had condemned the removal of public schools from church control in the Grand Duchy of Baden.

To see that this law was enforced "everywhere," McMaster sent a memorandum to Rome in 1874, asking whether Catholic parents might send their children to non-Catholic state schools, and whether Pius IX's letter to the Archbishop of Freiburg was applicable to the United States. In all, McMaster included fifteen points to clarify these two questions. The essence of his memorandum was that Catholics faced moral dangers in the public schools and that the bishops and priests had been ambiguous on the issue of refusing absolution to parents who placed their children in this danger.

In April 1874, acting on the memorandum sent by McMaster, the prefect of the Sacred Congregation of Propaganda de Fide in Rome sent a questionnaire to the bishops, expressing concern that Catholic youths were attending "public schools which are not subject to the vigilance and inspections of ecclesiastical authority."[22] This questionnaire asked why parents sent their children to public schools and how the matter of enforcing attendance at Catholic schools was being observed. The Bishops responded to Rome, which then issued the *Instruction of 1875.* The *Instruction* stated firmly that Catholic attendance at public schools was to be the exception, reserving that judgment to the bishop, and that denial of absolution was to be used to enforce attendance.

In the post-Civil War period, no one among the churchmen worked more avidly for a separate educational system than did Bishop Bernard McQuaid (1823–1909) of Rochester, New

York. "The battle for God's Church in this country has to be waged in the schoolroom," he stated, and he presented his views not only in writing, but by constructing a Catholic school system in his diocese.[23]

Announcing his intention to build up a system of "Christian Free Schools," McQuaid attempted to make non-Catholics see the injustice of the fact that Catholics were forced to support two systems. He noted that in the United States the idea of education was historically based on religious instruction; that the common-school notion emasculated education of all that gives it vitalizing power. In pursuing its aim of molding a common public out of the offspring of various European immigrants, McQuaid believed the public school system demanded that people become nonreligious. He stated it this way: "We have ceased to contend with Protestants, our battle is with indifference and disbelief."[24] He attempted to convince Protestants to join him in his campaign against the nonreligious public schools, and he attacked the endowment of colleges and universities as a demonstration of lack of concern for the poor. In so doing, McQuaid revealed his opinion that the school question involved more than the mere pitting of Protestant against Catholic—it involved rich against poor. Protestants, he warned, would be affected by secularization.

> While [Protestants] persist in attempting impossible things, the battle is going on in favor of indifferentism and infidelity. As the combat thickens, the third party [Catholics] withdraws quietly from the field, leaving evangelism to perish beneath the load of inconsistencies and fine philosophical theories which it chose to assume.[25]

McQuaid desired "a system of schools that embraced all the people while sacredly guarding the heaven-born rights of parents to control the instruction of their offspring."[26]

During the Third Plenary Council of Baltimore (1884),

Bishop McQuaid led the successful debate on the school question, stating that the church was losing members because of lack of schools, more than for any other reason, and that a decision to require Catholic schools would be "our surest guarantee of future growth and fixedness."[27]

Later, in reaction to John Ireland's NEA speech, McQuaid wrote Pope Leo XIII that the Bishop of Saint Paul had upset the peace that had come with the Baltimore Council III decision requiring Catholic schools. He foretold that any compromise with the state would end in complete sacrifice of Catholic education for children. There could be no accommodation on this issue unless the church disavowed the supernatural nature of religion: "Whenever the Catholic Church is ready to substitute the natural for the supernatural in religion, the time will have arrived for passing over our Schools to State control."[28]

McQuaid drew a clear line between the goals of Catholic schools and those of public schools. Catholic schools aimed to maintain a pure Catholic culture; public schools aimed to melt down and mix the various cultures in the United States. He warned of the indirect teaching of the public school and its moral atmosphere of indifference toward religious beliefs. He called it heresy, saying, "Indifferentism, with regard to all religions, ends in rank infidelity."[29]

In his letter to the Pope, McQuaid expressed concern about loss of contact with the sacraments and about intermarriage between Catholics and non-Catholics that association in the public school promoted. Finally, he expressed the opinion that the "thoughts and speech" of Catholics who attended the state schools "are tinctured with a liberalism that borders on infidelity."[30] Concluding his letter, McQuaid defended his belief that the church's mission was congruent with the conducting of schools—Catholic schooling was as necessary for the children as the church for their parents; the school was an instrument for the preaching of the gospel.

All during his struggle with John Ireland, McQuaid not only fought all efforts to change the Baltimore Council policy on Catholic education, but continued to develop parochial schools into a functioning system. He envisioned parochial high schools, Catholic colleges, Catholic residence centers on non-Catholic college campuses, a Catholic normal school, and teacher-training divisions in the motherhouses of the religious teaching orders. In 1871, attendance at McQuaid's schools in Rochester was 3,342; by 1893, it was 12,024.[31] In the nation, Catholic school attendance grew from 86,000 in 1860 to 850,000 in 1919.[32] As measured by the New York State Regents' exam, the intellectual progress of the students in McQuaid's schools far outdistanced those in Rochester's public schools. In 1896, McQuaid held the first diocesan institute for Catholic teachers, with an attendance of three hundred fifty nuns from various states. This meeting antedated the founding of the (National) Catholic Education Association by eight years.

## Thomism: The Twentieth-Century Spirit in Education

The twentieth century provided the setting for the development of the head to guide the body of Catholic education constructed in the nineteenth. In 1899 and 1907, in the encyclicals *Testem Benovolentiae* and *Pachendi,* Rome both confirmed the isolationist move and closed the bridges to the island by the condemnation of "Americanism" and "modernism," respectively. In 1897 Leo XIII's encyclical *Aeternis Patris* mandated a recovery of the thirteenth-century Thomistic philosophical synthesis of unity as an intellectual bulwark against the various forms of modernist thought that were splitting the world into separate religious and secular spheres.

William Halsey points out that under the influence of Thomism, Catholics in the United States came to the conclusion that there was a uniquely Catholic view of things —a rational and predictable cosmos, a moral structure inherent in the universe, and a belief in progress. This he identified as "American innocence."[33] Walter Ong makes the same point: "The American Catholic has lived the myth of America, but has hardly dared to speculate as to its meaning in relationship to his faith or to the spiritual interior life which this faith demands of him."[34]

Fayette Breaux Veverka demonstrates how the combination of nineteenth-century "American" physical establishment and twentieth-century "Roman" intellectual control produced a distinctive *theory* of Catholic education.[35] She elaborates three characteristics of twentieth-century Catholic education in the United States. First, it embodied a theological and educational vision that was truly public in that it wrestled with the relationship of faith to life, even if, for the most part, in its own island society. Second, the structure of Thomism gave Catholic education a sense of certitude during a period of sweeping social and cultural change. Third, the Catholic approach to religious education became institutionalized in the curriculum of Catholic schooling.

As the end result of the struggle between the two ideological camps, accommodation and isolation, and the emergence of neo-Thomism in the shape of the twentieth-century model of Catholic education, the structure of isolationism was reinforced with a separate system of schooling. However, because of the challenges it met, the goal of maintaining a pure Catholic culture (which this structure originally ought to cultivate) was transformed into the goal of "Americanizing" Catholics. Because this model of Catholic education resulted from a compromise, it represented neither the pure isolationist aims personified by McQuaid nor the accommodationist goals personified by Ireland. The eventual result was, to a great extent, not only unforeseen and unwished for by these two men and the camps they represented, but was, in many respects, contradictory to both McQuaid's desire for a pure Catholic culture and Ireland's wish for an engagement with the nation's society.

The Catholic Church's struggle with issues of religious tolerance, church polity, the relationship between church and state, and the relationship of religion to education produced a modus operandi for the twentieth century that established an island community, existing in its own complete world but completely surrounded by another.

Response to these four issues produced the mythos of Catholic schooling as the ideal form of Catholic education. The primary goal of Catholic education was the preservation of the Catholic faith. Its secondary goal, the interpretation of United States culture to the immigrants, took two competing directions: the creation of a pure Catholic culture, and the leavening of the nation's culture. Both these goals were responses to the issue of religious tolerance, and their particular characteristics illustrate a response to the other issues. First, the focus of the church's educational mission on universal education—that is, schooling—was a response to the relationship of religion to education. Second, the church's resistance to the state system of education responded to the relationship of church and state. Third, schools as *the* means to control the way Catholics related faith to culture also was a response to the relationship of church and state. Fourth, schools as the means to cultivate the laity's dependence on the clergy and the hierarchy responded to the issue of church polity.[36] Fifth, the schools as the means to "Americanize" Catholics under the control of the church was a response to religious tolerance.

## Conclusion: The Meaning of
## the Past for the Meaning of the Future

Was Catholic education privatized, or was it public religious education? This question can now be approached. The goals

91

of Catholic education and their characteristics, as set in the nineteenth century and lived out in the twentieth, did focus inward and were carried out within the prescribed boundaries of the island. But that island was *the* public world for a Catholic, a microcosm of the Holy Roman Empire of the thirteenth, the "greatest of centuries." The church attempted to create its own public society in the United States, and in this sense Catholic education was not merely domesticated but did become a "public" religious education in a particular people's isolated vision of the public.

Why did Catholic education come to be identified as Catholic schooling? Why is the agency of Catholic schooling losing its hold on the nation's Catholics? What will be the new mythos of the Catholic tradition in education? The story presented here has explored the first question. For the second, it is necessary to determine whether Catholic schools have performed the social and economic tasks of public education as effectively and efficiently as have the public schools; and whether, simultaneously, they have preserved and developed a distinctive Catholic identity.

The election in 1960 of the first Catholic to the highest office of the nation symbolized Catholic education's attainment of "Americanization." This, along with Vatican Council II's direct recognition of and engagement with modernity, suggests that the nineteenth- and twentieth-century aims of faith preservation and intellectual and cultural separation through ecclesiastically controlled schooling are no longer appropriate. Thus the Catholic Church in this country is free to reconstruct a new mythos (rationale and agencies) for Catholic education, to pick up the task that, according to Walter Ong, it turned away from one hundred years ago—the task of concentrating on the relationship of United States culture to the Catholic faith and to the spiritual interior life that faith demands.[37]

Being aware of the operative mentalities in the church's

educational mission and being able to examine these mentalities and analyze them as both results and causes of the social environment allows religious educators a cognitive way to intervene and shape the educational mission of the church. Such a method of study permits them to discover where and when the church lost its engagement with the public through the privitization, or domestication, of church education and thereby paves the way for a reconstruction of religious education as a public task.

In the case of Roman Catholics, both gifts and problems are brought to this issue of reconstruction. The gifts can be found in the uniqueness of the Catholic religious horizon. Langdon Gilkey points to several characteristics that animate Catholicism, as well as those that deaden it. Among the gifts are a sense of being a people, or a community; a moral responsiveness, or *caritas*; and a sacramental imagination. The problems, he points out, are the archaic and absolute structures that enshrine these gifts in a particular historical world-view and, by their intransigency, enslave Catholic minds, preventing them from seeking meaning. A transformed and radically reinterpreted Catholicism, says Gilkey, may serve "as the possible source or matrix for a creative modern Christianity."[38]

## Notes

1. James Hennessey, *American Catholics: A History of the Roman Catholic Community in the United States* (New York: Oxford University Press, 1981), p. 71.
2. Isaac T. Hecker, *The Church and the Age,* 10th ed. (New York: The Catholic Book Exchange, 1896).
3. Such a reaction was reinforced by the establishment of one of the most powerful religious societies in the church, the Jesuits, whose avowed aim was to defend the authority of the pope.
4. Hecker, *The Church and the Age,* pp. 197-98, 204-5, 199-200.
5. Walter J. Ong, *American Catholic Crossroads* (New York: Macmillan Co., 1959), p. 48.

6. Jacobean liberalism, spawned from the excesses of the French Revolution, possessed an inherent anticlericalism.

7. Actually, the isolationists employed a more authoritarian style than Rome in ruling the church during the period of immigration.

8. Peter Guilday, *The Life and Times of John Carroll: Archbishop of Baltimore, 1735–1815,* 2 vols. (New York: Encyclopedia Press, 1922), vol. 1, pp. 384-85.

9. In an address to the U.S. Congress, January 8, 1826, England declared, "We do not profess to believe our Pope to be infallible." Cf. Leon Le Buffe, "Tensions in American Catholicism, 1820–1870, An Intellectual History" (Ph.D. diss., Catholic University of America, 1973), p. 39.

10. Neil G. McCluskey, *Catholic Education in America: A Documentary History* (New York: Bureau of Publications, Teachers College, Columbia University, 1964), pp. 128, 130, citing John Ireland, *The Church and Modern Society,* 2nd ed. (Chicago: D. H. McBride, 1896).

11. Ibid., p. 133.

12. Ireland, *Church and Modern Society,* pp. 58-59.

13. Ibid., p. 64.

14. Ibid., p. 234.

15. Cited in James M. McDonnell, "Orestes A. Brownson: Catholic Schools, Public Schools, and Education," in *An American Church,* ed. David J. Alvarez (Moraga, Calif.: St. Mary's College, 1979), p. 152.

16. Ibid., p. 153.

17. McCluskey, *Catholic Education in America,* pp. 101-2.

18. Ibid., p. 110.

19. Michael B. Katz, ed., *Education in American History: Readings on the Social Issues* (New York: Praeger, 1973), p. 44.

20. Jerome E. Diffley, "Catholic Reaction to American Public Education, 1792–1852" (Ph.D. diss., University of Notre Dame, 1959), p. 235.

21. Thomas T. McAvoy, "Public Schools and James McMaster," *Review of Politics* 28 (January 1966):22.

22. Bernard J. Meiring, "Educational Aspects of the Legislation of the Councils of Baltimore" (Ph.D. diss., University of California, Berkeley, 1963), p. 145.

23. Norlene Mary Kunkle, "Bishop Bernard J. McQuaid and Catholic Education" (Ph.D. diss., University of Notre Dame, 1974), p. 130.

24. Frederick J. Zwierlein, *The Life and Letters of Bishop McQuaid,* 3 vols. (Rochester, N.Y.: The Art Print Shop, 1925–1927), vol. 1, p. 139.

25. Ibid., p. 130.

26. Ibid., p. 132.

27. Kunkle, "Bishop Bernard J. McQuaid," p. 238.

28. Zwierlein, *Life and Letters of Bishop McQuaid,* vol. 3, pp. 191-93.

29. Ibid.

30. Ibid.

31. Ibid., vol. 2, p. 324.

32. Edgar P. McCarren, "The Origin and Early Years of the National Catholic Educational Association" (Ph.D. diss., Catholic University of America, 1966), p. 256.

33. William H. Halsey, *The Survival of American Innocence: Catholicism in an Era of Disillusionment, 1920–1940* (Notre Dame: University of Notre Dame Press, 1980).

34. Walter J. Ong, *Frontiers in American Catholicism* (New York: Macmillan Co., 1957), p. 125.

35. Fayette Breaux Veverka, "Defining a Catholic Approach to Education in the United States, 1920–1950," paper delivered to the Association of Professors and Researchers in Religious Education, Anaheim, Calif. (November 1983). See Veverka, "For God and Country: Catholic Schooling in the 1920's" (Ed.D. diss., Teachers College, Columbia University, 1982) for a most complete analysis of the foundations of twentieth-century Catholic education.

36. Gary Wills shows how Catholic schooling affected church polity: "The problem of building, equipping, and operating this church-school complex formed a body of priests who advanced toward their monsignorate, their bishopric, by virtue of business skill. The most successful bishop was the one who had opened more schools than any other—Spellman was the champion on the East Coast, McIntyre on the West Coast" (*Bare Ruined Choirs: Doubt, Prophecy, and Radical Religion* [Garden City, N.Y.: Doubleday & Co., 1972], pp. 23-24).

37. Ong, *Frontiers in American Catholicism*, p. 125.

38. Langdon Gilkey, *Catholicism Confronts Modernity: A Protestant View* (New York: Seabury Press, 1975), p. 15.

# Education and Public Paideia: The Progressive Vision of Religious Education

PROTESTANT religious educators entered the twentieth century with a clear sense of destiny. Not only was the new century to be *The Christian Century,* as the editors of the new journal declared, but reform of the church's educational program was to fulfill the church's destiny. Most religious educators agreed that the church was the soul of the educational system. It was to supplement with moral and religious spirit the intellectual and manual education of the public school.

While the more perceptive knew that the nineteenth-century partnership was dissolving, all looked for ways Protestant church education could continue to complement public education. For example, George Albert Coe, one of the first professors of religious education, declared at the 1910 meeting of the Religious Education Association (REA) that "future generations in this country will be trained in religion by the churches or not at all."[1] His words reflect the growing awareness that the church needed to improve its educational program.

Here then is both the hope and the challenge for Protestant education in the early twentieth century: It was necessary to the grand scheme of education in the United States, and it needed to improve significantly to fulfill its purpose. The educators sought to rebuild links between the church's education and the other educational agencies of the public: schools, voluntary associations, and means of public information and public livelihood.

While nineteenth-century Protestant educators had been concerned with forming the character of the nation itself, in the early twentieth century they assumed that democracy was both the ideology and the strategy of education. These reformers, the progressive religious educators, desired to place the church's education on a foundation as solid as that of public education. They sought to institutionalize patterns of church influence. Their efforts demonstrate a continuing commitment of the church to the public, but they also demonstrate the continuing domestication of church education.

### The Ideology of Progressive Religious Education: Reestablishing the Church in a Democratic Paideia

It is said that progressive church educators were embarrassed by the pedagogic quality of the Sunday school and that they attempted to upgrade educational standards and professionalize the teaching of religion. While this is true, the rationale for their efforts goes deeper than a concern for quality. Empowered by a sense of urgency, they sought to reestablish a significant place for Protestant education in the public of the United States. Motivated by the rapid social change, the disintegration of the Protestant concensus in public life, and the increased confusion in the culture, they proclaimed out of a sense of social imperative, as had Coe, that it was intolerable for "the fragmentary opportunities that our Sunday schools now have [to] be largely frittered away through slipshod organization and methods."[2] Protestant education needed both expansion and improvement in order to participate as a full partner in democracy. Ominous feelings of social disruption caused by the First World War and economic anxiety further reinforced their efforts.

The educators believed that the church was necessary for the preservation of democracy, and this essential relationship was clearly articulated in the first publications of the International Sunday School Council of Religious Education, founded in 1922. The Education Committee of the council defined the age as one of emergency for Protestant education. Spiritual illiteracy was thought to be pervasive and a clear menace to democratic life. In fact, the members of the committee agreed that the church was failing as a teacher of spiritual, moral, and religious instruction, and thus the United States was changing, with no apparent moral and religious sensitivities.[3]

To signal its commitment to the future of democracy in the United States, the International Council endorsed a 1921 resolution of the National Council of Education as their platform:

> In view of the dependence of democracy upon religion, and the attacks to which all churches and democratic governments are alike being subjected by radicals and emissaries of nations under radical control: it is the duty of all churches, irrespective of differences of creed, to unite in an effort to make religious education more universal and efficient, to emphasize democratic elements in religious instruction, and to correlate religious instruction with all elements in public school education helpful to religion . . . and it is the duty of churches and public schools alike to make earnest effort to ensure a more general reverence for divinity and respect for all things religious.[4]

The belief that spiritual ideas and democratic virtues must be promoted together inspired their rhetoric and action. Hugh Magill, the new general secretary of the International Council and a former field secretary for the National Education Association, stated the conviction forcefully: In addition to "bringing the gospel of truth to every soul," the task of the church was now "supplemented by the patriotic motive of instilling in the hearts and minds of the American youth those religious principles which give sanction and support to the moral elements necessary to good citizenship, and the preservation of free government."[5]

These powerful statements reveal an acceptance of the ideology of democratic education on the part of progressive educators. They no longer sought to form the ideology, as had Bushnell, but now assumed it and sought to find in it a place for the church. Their books and articles focused on the relation of the church's education to democracy in the United States and the attempt to establish an equal partnership of church and public education.[6]

The theses of their writings clearly reflected the new situation in education. Progressive religious educators realized that church and culture were no longer in a supportive symbiotic relationship. Several spoke of the way secularization, industrialization, pluralism, and increasing individualism had changed the character of education in the United States. They feared that questions of morality, human ideals, and proper forms of social life were being ignored. Henry Cope, the executive secretary of the REA, represented the feelings of many of his colleagues when he criticized public schooling for losing a moral conscience:

> We have been so intensely practical that we have developed the menacing machine of educated workers who have the power of the engine and none of the wisdom of the engineer, who can run factories and great systems of business but lack either wisdom or power to run themselves. They know where they can make business go but no one knows where they will drive themselves, nor whither they may drift.[7]

Cope and others pleaded for a balancing of secular with the religious, so that education itself could be understood as "a process of the directed development of life into fullness for the sake of the full and efficient life of common service."[8] They described the immense problem created by the separation of church and state and by the development of dual but complementary systems of church and public schools. While accepting the historic principle of separation, these progressives argued that there had been unintended consequences. William Clayton Bower probably stated these consequences most starkly. He maintained that the exclusion of religion from the schools had distorted and dismembered the cultural inheritance for children and youth. Persons were coming to know themselves without their religious heritage. Moreover, this situation seriously jeopardized democracy itself, for citizens were not learning the most fundamental resources for democracy's maintenance.

> Democracy can scarcely hope to compete with these aggressive forms of totalitarianism [represented in facism and communism] unless it can evoke wholehearted commitments to the Four Freedoms that are essential to the good life for the common man. In the judgment of many, these values are in their deepest nature profoundly religious and Christian in their implications. In these fundamental and comprehending values of the good life for all lie at once the cohesive force of the democratic state and its dynamic.[9]

The concern for improving the educational quality of the church's program, then, became a concern for supporting the ideology of democracy in the United States and the role of religion in democracy's continuing development. Walter Athearn of Boston University, chairperson of the Committee on Education of the International Council, provided a description of the church's task which captivated the council.

He argued that the church and the public school were two parallel arenas in the educational system.[10] Together, they completed the arch of education with the highest educational principles, competent organizations, excellent teachers, and a sympathetic relationship. Lacking either, education was inadequate and incomplete.

Yet here was the problem they sensed: Many who worked in church education seemed to have neither the inclination nor the educational resources to fulfill the church's responsibilities. Despite their rhetoric, church educators seemed more concerned with the internal life of the church than with its public role. Some, like Bower, sensed the domestication of church education. It seemed the "priest of the *status quo*" more than a social leader.[11] Church leaders had not seemed to realize that the homogeneous society of the nineteenth century had dissolved and that the church needed to develop new resources for both education and ministry. One commentator, Arthur Cushman McGiffert, the president of Union Theological Seminary and also president of the Religious Education Association, argued that the church had abdicated its teaching function, which had been taken over by other agencies of modern society—the press, the public school, the women's club, and the lecture platform.[12] The plea of progressive educators was for the church to recover and resume that function, which they felt would not only foster democracy but critically reform church and society.

It was necessary to reconstruct church education in order for it to fulfill what was perceived as its accepted role in public life. In concept, most of these educators sought to balance the spiritual task of the church and its commitment to democracy. For example, Bower declared:

> Most of all, vital religion needs to discover techniques for subjecting our contemporary civilization—its science, its

machines, its industry and its democratic way of life—to criticism, evaluation and reconstruction, in terms of these spiritual values. This has always been and still is the function of prophetic religion.[13]

His frustration lay in the fact that the resources for remaking the church and society had been made available in the potential coalescence of the new social interpretation of religion, the new science of education, and the emerging social sciences, yet they were rarely used.[14] The best progressive educators, however, did attempt to relate these factors and, in so doing, remake religious education so that it could be faithful to its task.

Thus the progressive religious educators intended to enhance the role of the church in the culture in a new epoch. They realized that the church had played a substantial role in a previous homogeneous society and that the relationship of church and culture should be renewed. Most thought that improvement of the church's institutions of education would enable people to value the church's tradition and vocation, as well as the culture's life and institutions.

## Progressive Strategies of the Church in Public Education

In contrast to the nineteenth century when the task was perceived as forming the nation's paideia of education, progressives now essentially assumed the democratic paideia and therefore expended their effort on constructing strategies. Two proposals were predominant: (1) to remake the Sunday school into an effective school of the church, parallel in competence, professionalism, and form to the public school; and (2) to coordinate church agencies for education on the national scene. Both strategies focused on accomplishments within the church to improve education in religion.

## The Church School

The first and most widely accepted strategy was the development of the church school. Such an approach trusted the educational revolution taking place in the public school, with its bureaucratic definition of educational form, and sought to emulate it.

The church school strategy initially was based on the assumption that the failure of the church to adequately fulfill its educational responsibilities was due to the inadequacy of its educational program. If the church school could be graded, organized, and professionalized like the public school, the progressives felt it could again become a crucial force in the nation's education.

They looked to the public school, thinking that its goals were set and that the dream of universal education was becoming a reality. The common school, in their minds, had achieved a truly public character. Research in child psychology had resulted in a graded curriculum; school management was developing into a science, applying principles of corporate bureaucracy; school buildings that were more functional were being designed. Progressive religious educators therefore called for parallel progress in the church's educational efforts.[15] In particular, they called for graded curriculum, more adequate means of teacher preparation, new educational buildings for the church, and efficient methods of church school organization.

In terms of content, educators sought to transcend the exclusive reliance of the Sunday school on the nineteenth-century Uniform Lesson biblical curriculum. Research in developmental psychology had convinced them that content needed to be sequenced in terms of psychological and cognitive development, and related to everyday life experiences. The curriculum they generated was graded in content, focusing on God's love in the early elementary classes, the heroes of the faith for older elementary, a decision for faith in the junior-high years, and on how one should live as a member of the church for the senior-high students.[16]

Moreover, the progressives were concerned about the lack of coordination and unity in the church's efforts at education. Their research had revealed that within the church, a variety of agencies competed, overlapped, and drained energy from one another.[17] They sought means to relate these educational efforts—Sunday schools, children's programs, youth societies, men's and women's organizations—into a comprehensive and coordinated church school, educationally coextensive with the life of the congregation.

The church school of the progressive educator was to reflect the pedagogic innovations of public education and coordinate the agencies of the church's educational ministry, building on the model of the public school. The congregational committee on education and the professional director of religious education were the two innovations suggested in order to create the church school: The committee was to be the parallel of the local school board; the director, the principal or superintendent. By 1913 both were included in the standards set by the REA to judge effectiveness in local church education.[18] The job of the committee was to survey educational needs, adopt curriculum, provide facilities, select teachers, supervise the total educational program, and select a director of religious education who, in turn, would supervise the church school and train its teachers. In this manner, progressive educators hoped to enhance the quality of church education for the public.

## A Church and Community Program of Education

By the middle of the second decade, church educators began to celebrate their progress, but they also realized that by itself, the strategy of the local church school would not be effective. More was needed to achieve unity. They searched for ways religious education could have more effect on the total community. Their first effort involved religious education related to the schools. Later they developed a design for community programs of religious education.

Early experimentation in weekday religious education at places such as Gary, Indiana, and Malden, Massachusetts, gave the progressive religious educators hope.[19] Their efforts were led by Walter Athearn, who, in *Religious Education and American Democracy* (1917), definitively described a unified system of education in the United States:

> This will require the establishing of a system of church schools which will parallel the public schools all the way from the kindergarten to the university. These two systems of schools must be closely coordinated in the interest of a unified educational program, which will guarantee to every child both intelligence and godliness.[20]

Most of the progressive educators concurred with Athearn's assessment that the unification of the educational system for "intelligence and godliness" was the task of the churches.[21] The school itself, they believed, would not take this responsibility, but would respond to initiatives of the church.

In 1922 the International Sunday School Association united with the Sunday School Council of Evangelical Denominations to form the International Council of Religious Education. This move enabled the organization to function as a coordinating structure, capable of relating denominational and interdenominational church organizations into a national, parallel program of religious instruction.[22] Such a system would encompass three levels of education: (1) schools—church school, weekday religious education, church colleges, and graduate schools of religion; (2) training institutions—local church teacher-training efforts, community training schools, departments of religious education in church colleges, and graduate schools of religious education; and (3) educational supervision—local church, community agencies of religious education, denominational and international religious education organizations.[23] The hope was that such a system would allow each church and locale, as well as the nation itself, to survey the religious educational needs of the community, coordinate church effort, and provide a competent system of religious instruction.

The advocates of the community system realized that they must have power and a comprehensive program to lead the community and the nation. A bureaucratically coordinated national program of religious education seemed the most adequate solution for reasserting the educational power of the church in an increasingly pluralistic age. The resolution adopted by the International Sunday School Association in 1918 reflected the seriousness of these progressives: "The price which the American people must pay for religious liberty is whatever sum may be required to erect and operate a dual system of schools. . . . This system, when finally developed and unified, will provide for the American people the most complete program of universal education which the world has ever known."[24]

## Assessment

In their search to recover the role of the church in public life, progressive religious educators sought to improve the quality of the church school and to coordinate, on a community and national basis, the various agencies of the church's education. While recognizing that relations between church and culture had changed, they were confident that the church could again find and fulfill its responsibility. They sought to provide the church with the competence to undertake this task and enough power to again be a factor in public life.

Yet in hindsight, it is clear that the progressives' strategies continued the domestication of church education. At most, they improved the churches' education of church people and thus continued to restrict church education to the household of the faith. But the fundamental relationship of church and culture was not addressed.

To understand this domestication, it is necessary to look at two factors: (1) Church education was subordinated to public schooling and the ecology of the education of the public was ignored; and (2) a commitment to public life was confused with a focus on individual religious development.

First, while the liberal progressives were well aware that education took place through means other than schooling, they became caught up in the excitement around the public school and its triumphal attempt to include all education within its boundaries. Most of the educators heard and concurred with Bower's reminder that the whole community educates through its whole life—schools, motion pictures, other media, and political processes.[25] Many bemoaned the fact that so many children and adults were outside the arena of the church and therefore usually beyond the church's reach. In particular, they continued to repeat the judgment that a child spent only twenty minutes a day in religious instruction, while spending a significant amount of time in school and the rest in the library, in play, and in family and community activities.[26] To respond, they chose the bureaucratic approach of the public school and spoke primarily about coordinating activities within the church. The progressives' practice thus domesticated their rhetoric.

The fact is that they acted as if a national organization would achieve their ends and as if schooling alone were sufficient to educate a people. They quickly discovered, however, that a national system of religious education could command neither the respect of the nation nor the resources to achieve its grand design. The respective agendas of individual denominations, the fact that it was easier to coordinate elements within a local church than between churches, and the economic upheaval of the Great Depression—all blocked the dream of a comprehensive national program.[27] In many ways, by focusing on the church and school relationship, they moved beyond the limited heritage bequeathed to them by the Sunday school movement, but their efforts were insufficient to discover a significant place for church education in the education of the public.

Moreover, their tendency to concentrate on the development of the individual redirected energies that could have centered on a social agenda. Uniformly throughout the literature, progressive educators argued that the contemporary concept of personality required that the individual be understood in a social context.[28] For this reason they demanded new curriculum that dealt with life development instead of relying exclusively on biblical knowledge. Yet their actions did not adequately address the interaction of the individual and the social environment. In many ways this is not surprising, for a major impetus to progressive religious education had been the application of the child-study movement to the church, the recovery of the concept of Christian nurture, and the push for graded curriculum. Most of the progressives were unable to maintain a dual commitment to the person and to the social environment.

The rhetoric of many progressives had been inspired by the social gospel movement. They fully agreed that conversion was limited as a metaphor for education because of its exclusive focus on the individual; yet they in turn continued to domesticate the social gospel perspective. For example, the social gospel contrasted conversion with social life to clarify the social agenda of the church; progressive educators substituted a contrast between conversion and nurture.[29] That replacement reveals that the progressive vision was confined to the formation of Christian persons within the church, since nurture restricts education to the Christian community. The power of the external social environment to orient a person to reality and to limit the social role of the church thus is likely to be overlooked. Liberal Christian educators today are still heirs of the shift from social life to nurture, and unless the metaphor of nurture is challenged, Christian education will continue to miss its role in the wider educational ecology.

Progressive educators were committed to a public role for church education, and they were aware of the intimate relation of the church's education to the culture's education. But their strategies did not effect a more adequate public role for church education, since they neither reestablished the church in the forming of the public paideia nor placed the church effectively in the culture's educational ecology.[30] The work of progressives emphasized individual development and church life, rather than social reconstruction and the nation's conscience.

## Clues for the Future

How, then, can the domestication of church education be transcended? Are there effective theories and strategies of Christian religious education appropriate to a new pluralistic culture? Within the progressive movement itself are two educators who provide glimpses of new possibilities: George Albert Coe and William Clayton Bower. By focusing more comprehensively on the relationship of the church to the education of the public, both Coe and Bower saw some of the limitations of the progressive strategies. They were aware that the relationship of church to culture had changed radically since the nineteenth-century formulation of Protestant education. The church, in their view, was not functioning as a significant force in shaping the public; instead, it had conformed to the culture. Their concern was to recover the critical and prophetic role of religion; the church's education therefore needed to transcend traditional practice and directly interrelate the religious with the social environment.

The biographies of Coe and Bower illustrate the breadth of their commitments as well as their expansion of the progressive vision. Although they led in the development of the discipline of religious education, neither received the comprehensive hearing he deserved. The progressive strategies were so embedded that alternatives were often unconsciously translated into traditional practice and thereby lost their power to reform.

Throughout most of his career, Coe was the primary spokesperson for academic interests in religious education.[31] From teaching positions at Northwestern University and Union Theological Seminary, Coe sought to integrate an educational theory represented by a creative extension of John Dewey's analysis of the relation of the individual to the culture, with psychological research on the nature of religious experience and religious community. He was recognized by his contemporaries as a prophet of the reconstruction of both religion and education.[32] The end of all education, Coe believed, was ethics; therefore he committed himself to reform of the school, the church, and the society. His convictions involved him in such causes as woman's rights, the fight against racism, and the critique of capitalism. Despite these commitments, his own work in religious education remained primarily theoretical. Only rarely did he offer practical tools to effect his social agenda, and therefore his ideas about reconstruction often lost their power when others translated them into practice.

In Coe's opinion, only through religious education could the goals of social life be related to people's yearning for wholeness and transformation. For example, he argued that

religious education is not a part of general education, it *is* general education. It is the whole of which our so-called secular education is only a part or phrase. Religious education alone takes account of the whole personality, of all its powers, all its duties, all its possibilities, and of the ultimate reality of the environment.[33]

This commitment to a religious education that involved the whole of education and transcended its restriction to the church is probably best reflected in Coe's move, five years before retirement, to Teacher's College in New York. From his retirement in 1927 until his death in 1952, Coe continued to prod the church about its educational task and work for social change.

William Clayton Bower, after pastorates in Indiana, New York, and California, entered upon a distinguished academic career in religious education at Transylvania College and the College of the Bible in Lexington, Kentucky, and at the Divinity School of the University of Chicago.[34] Throughout his one hundred four years, Bower attempted to unite the Christian religion and contemporary culture. It was in education that he believed this connection could best be made, for it was in education that the experience of the individual met the culture. It was the forum where the traditions of a people, their religious and moral aspirations, their individual freedom and their corporateness, became related. Therefore he felt that education stimulated cultural and personal advancement, was democratic, was inspired by religious values, and was accepting of new knowledge and change.[35]

Bower embodied these commitments in his attempts to reclaim the religious in all of education. He not only worked to advance the church, but participated in educational efforts throughout the society—as a member of the Lexington school board, a leader of the Religious Education Association and the International Council of Religious Education, a delegate to the 1940 White House Conference on Children in a

Democracy, and as the chairman of the advisory committee of the Kentucky Program of Moral and Spiritual Values. Although he knew that education encompasses more than schooling, Bower's own efforts focused on the relationship of church and state in public education. He was convinced that this mission was "most crucial and urgent in a culture in which amazing advances have been made in scientific knowledge and technology, but in which there is a cultural lag in the realm of values—religion, ethics, and art."[36]

Both Coe and Bower sought to transform the relationship of religion to education. Coe, for example, argued that the primary meaning and contribution of any vital religion was "at the precarious edge of life and civilization."[37] Bower concurred, arguing that the church was the only institution in modern life that could critically assess the drift of society and provide the vision and impetus for social reconstruction.[38] Both educators sought to understand why the church had been captured by the culture and the prophetic voice of religion lost. On the whole, they agreed on two reasons: (1) The church had tended to ignore significant cultural changes and uncritically accepted their impact; and (2) the school as educator of the public had been increasingly cut off from the ideals, cultural inheritance, and method provided in religion.[39] Fundamentally, both men then sought to remake religion and education; for as Coe concluded, the church without a social vision and the school without a religious vision are both inadequate.[40]

### Beyond Domestication—On Remaking Religion

"We need a fellowship of repentence, of radical self-commitment, of faith and hope that dare the utmost."[41] With words like these Coe began his analysis of the role of religion in society. The church was the "mother of radicalism" and the companion of those who sought humanization. Similarly, for

Bower the church was "the means for the continued reorientation of one's life, for self-criticism, for the rectification of values and for commitment to the causes of the Kingdom of God."[42] The task for church education, they felt, was first to clarify the role of religion in the changing culture, and second, to seek to be faithful to that new responsibility.

The function of religion in society was thus a primary question.[43] Building on the insights of both psychology and sociology, Coe and Bower viewed the individual as being formed in interaction with the social world. His or her own person is transformed and grows through experiences with the physical world, with the world of other persons and institutions, with the world of traditions, and with the cosmic world.

In this anthropological theory lies the basis of their understanding of religion and religious formation. Religion was seen as central to the cultural heritage of the people. It provided them with ideals, values, modes of ethical conduct, and procedures for social living. Religion was thus crucial to the formation of the individual personality and the social life. It provided critical awareness for decision making, in light of eternity.

Both Bower and Coe tended to avoid the metaphysical questions of the "truth" of religion and the meaning of revelation, concentrating instead on the empirical presence and contribution of religion in the social fabric. They feared that children were growing up and that society was changing without a significant interaction with the ideals of sacredness of personality, ultimate nature of reality, and kingdom of God as models for social living. Because the church seemed not to understand the culture, it was not providing the critical principle necessary for human social formation. Consequently, through their interaction with the social fabric, persons were being subtly coerced into accepting consumerism, capitalism, elite understandings of humanity, and war.

Religion therefore functioned within a social matrix. Yet Coe and Bower saw that the sectarianism of most religious persons caused them to focus their concern on clarifying sectarian beliefs and fighting for ascendency. Such a pattern continued to restrict religion to the churches, missing the essential responsibility of religion to assist in the construction of society. While Coe did not question the concept of voluntarism, he argued that as voluntary associations, churches must look beyond themselves and their bickering to engage "the great social problems of individual destiny."[44] He seems not to have realized that voluntarism itself stimulates homogeneous church entities in the society, each separately vying for its own cause and people.

Nevertheless, Coe and Bower suggest to us that the central issue for Christian religious education is the discernment of the function of religion in the society. It is an issue of church and culture. Without question, as Coe argued, religion is an essential factor in the formation of the public mind (paideia): "Organized religion in this part of the world includes ideas and thought-processes that concern some at least of the interests of any mind that can be called public."[45]

Second, not only must the function of religion be discerned, but those actual entities which carry the religion, the churches, must be expressly faithful. Coe was convinced that the failure of church education was due in great part to lack of religion in the church.[46] Without a visible, faithful church, religious education had very little chance of being effective. Bower agreed, maintaining that people need to participate "in a group or groups in which religious attitudes are vitally operative" in providing a world-view "capable of kindling the imagination, evoking the emotions and enlisting whole-hearted devotion" to principles of the sacredness of the personality and the kingdom of God.[47] The commitment of both educators is reflected in these words of Coe: "A church that is not actively in the struggle against repression and for complete liberation of the public mind has no valid claim to being different from the 'world.'"[48]

Both Bower and Coe called for social life to continue as an actual agenda of the church's education. Issues of labor unrest, peace, capitalism, human rights, the use of power, and social experience were to be the intrinsic content of the church's activity and its education. They felt continuing research was needed to find ways the Christian religion could function in the public world. But even while this research was being carried on, the church needed to *be* the church in debates over the shape of public life. They called the church to remake itself beyond a community that dealt only with its own internal life, to recover its prophetic, world-shaping responsibility.

Embedded in the thought of these two educators was the conviction that religion is intrinsic to the social process. It is essential to the determination of the parts of a culture that are to be transmitted and transformed, and the way this is to be accomplished. Religion provides the paideia of a culture's education with the dimension of depth. While they missed the essential relationship between voluntarism and the failure of the churches' education, their legacy urges the church to find patterns for injecting the religious into cultural decisions and for faithfully embodying the call of the religious in life.

## Beyond Church Schooling— On Remaking the Educational Ecology

Bower and Coe sought to expand the strategies of education in the United States. They understood education in a comprehensive fashion, as those broad cultural processes by which a person, as well as the social fabric, is formed and reformed.[49] The child, for example, was understood to be educated by personal interaction within the family, the culture, the school, the church, the peers, and so on. But how does religion clarify its role in this broad educational matrix so that it can become one of the vital factors by which personality is formed? Or in Bower's words, How are the resources of religion made available?

It would be excessive to say that Bower and Coe articulated an educational ecology which clarified the churches' inter-action within the network of educational institutions. Both spent most of their effort on only two elements in the ecology—the church and the public school. However, they realized that not only was the culture restricting the church's role, but that the church itself was restricting its educational effect. Bower fought the limiting of religious education to an ecclesial task for the church's members; he concluded it was ultimately self-defeating. He believed that church efforts in the church school, and even in weekday church schools, failed because they maintained the separation of religion from education, perpetuated sectarianism, and did not reach the entire populace. He was convinced that any adequate alternative needed to be based "upon a well-considered philosophy regarding the nature of education, the nature of religion, and the relation of church and state."[50] Such a relation is precisely what he attempted in the Kentucky Program of Moral and Spiritual Values. His purpose was to provide procedures to relate the community of the school and its curriculum to moral and spiritual values, to provide teachers with skills in guiding and sensitizing pupils to values, and to enable pupils to form and enact value-filled lives.[51]

While their own work focused primarily on the church and school and, to a lesser degree, on the family, the two progressives did not ignore the educational responsibilities of the total community. Bower is particularly illustrative as he lists school, church, family, and "other social agencies" as educative institutions, claiming that

> education in all its forms, including that having to do with religious nurture, is an affair of the community and not of any

116

single institutions. . . . There is imperative need, therefore, that the base of education shall be drawn in the total life of the community. Around this *new center* of education it becomes the responsibility of the whole community to sit down before the needs of its children and young people, including their religious needs, and ask what it is that each agency has to contribute to a comprehensive and co-ordinated program of education for the whole self and for the whole community.[52]

By "new center," Bower meant that the church could no longer focus only on its own curriculum and procedures, but must make a commitment to education in the wider culture. It must engage the variety of agencies that dealt with education and must stimulate public conversation about their interaction and curriculum. Coe and Bower thus fought all efforts to restrict the education of the church to the church school.[53]

Moreover, they sought to articulate a teaching method that involved the interaction of religious faith with the culture. Coe called it "creative education that is likewise Christian." The role of cultural experience in growth was central to both men. Education should enable people to analyze the content of experience in light of cultural and religious heritages (the past) and in anticipation of God's continuing creation process as reflected in the vision of the Kingdom (the future).[54] Only in this manner could the experience of persons then be reconstructed. An added benefit would be that the church and the society would themselves be reconstructed in the process.

Bower articulated the elements of such a process for both church and public education. His model can be summarized in five steps: (1) Assist persons to reflect objectively on the actual situations they face in life experience; (2) help persons reconstruct and understand the experience in terms of their own past experience; (3) guide persons to understand the experience in terms of the cultural heritage of the religious group and the society; (4) engage these reflections with one another, searching for meanings, values, possible responses, and outcomes; and (5) decide upon the action or behavior that should be adopted.[55] Both educators felt the teaching method should provide the interaction of experience, heritage, and emergence of God—all amidst the variety of factors and agencies that form persons.

Both Coe and Bower looked upon education as being fundamentally the task of the whole community, seeking to understand the experiences people confront, exploring the resources for meaning and decision making available in the traditions of the community, and acting to create new meaning and behaviors in the midst of the community's life. Therefore the educational ecology needs to be understood and its interactions publicly clarified. But moreover, through the teaching of the religious tradition, persons need to be given the tools to exist in the world. Religion and community life thus continue to be dynamic processes of encountering the new, recovering the cultural heritage, and creating new meaning in the actual experience of life.

## Conclusion

The purpose of the progressive religious educators was to renew and re-image religious education in a changing cultural scene. Their search for a new approach is also our search. As Bower and Coe emphasized, the church needs to claim its role in the educational ecology, and people must be given skills to negotiate faith and cultural experience.

The clues of those educators may be fruitful in our own reflection. First, they call the church to assess its role, since churches cannot be separated from the culture but are an intrinsic part of it. The church can affect the public world only by understanding, claiming, and expanding its actual ways of entry into the culture. The insight of the progressives reveals that the educational ministry of the church is reflective of the role of the church in society. Without awareness, its goals and strategies tend to be restricted to the cultural definitions of the church and the prevailing patterns of education in the culture. The situation reflects the thought of Paul Tillich in his *Theology of Culture:*

> The problem of the Church School is more than the problem of a particular educational aim. It is the problem of the relation of Christianity and culture generally and Christianity and education especially. The problem is infinite and must be solved again in every generation.[56]

Our present task is to understand the possibilities of the church and its education in the culture—to determine how the Word can be taught and preached so that it can be understood; to make the church a center of meaning, value, and purpose; and to effect personal and social transformation.

Second, Bower and Coe call us to recognize the ecology within which the education of the public takes place. But recognition is not sufficient; people must also acquire skills in negotiating the ecology and relating to its various aspects. We must expand our notion of education and work to help people understand how meanings are made in culture, to empower people to function as receivers and creators of meaning. As a primary meaning-making institution, the church's education is particularly suited to this task.

Such is the heritage that has been left us by the best of the progressive educators—a heritage that calls for the church to claim its public responsibility, and for church education to provide people with the tools to understand the educational ecology within which they find themselves, as well as the methods to transform the perspectives they encounter into meanings and decisions for living. Coe and Bower sought to understand the pathways an individual must travel to become Christian and the actual function of the church in culture.

Their commitments, as ours may be, were to understand the ecology and to provide means of traversing it.

There has been a consistent thrust in Protestant education to engage the public; yet factors have interfered to simplify the goal inappropriately and to narrow its form to the school of the church. When we recognize these possibilities and tensions, as well as the enduring domestication, we will have begun to set a viable Christian education policy for the future.

## Notes

1. George Albert Coe, "The President's Annual Address: New Reasons for Old Duties," *Religious Education* 5 (April 1910):4.
2. Ibid., p. 5.
3. *Report of Committee on Education* (Kansas City: International Sunday School Council of Religious Education [ISSCRE], 1922), p. 11.
4. Ibid.
5. Hugh S. Magill, "A Comprehensive Program of Education, Secular and Religious," in *Organized Sunday School Work, 1918–1922, Official Report of the 16th International Sunday School Convention,* ed. Herbert H. Smith (Chicago: ISSCRE, 1922), p. 162.
6. Some of the most interesting of the books and articles are Walter S. Athearn, *Religious Education and American Democracy* (Boston: Pilgrim Press, 1917); idem, "Protestantism's Contribution to Character Building in a Democracy," *International Journal of Religious Education* 2 (June 1926):26-29; William Clayton Bower, "Making the Resources of Religion Available in Education," *Religious Education* 36 (January–March 1941):3-8; idem, "The White House Conference on Children in a Democracy," *Religious Education* 35 (April 1940):76-82; George Albert Coe, "The Nature of Discipline for Democracy," *Religious Education* 14 (June 1919):136-47; idem, "Let Us Rethink the Purpose of Religious Education," *Religious Education* 23 (December 1928):974-78; Henry F. Cope, *Education for Democracy* (New York: Macmillan Co., 1920); idem, "Democratic Training Through the Church," *Religious Education* 13 (December 1918):401-11.
7. Cope, *Education for Democracy*, p. 54.
8. Ibid., pp. 55-56.
9. William Clayton Bower, *Church and State in Education* (Chicago: University of Chicago Press, 1941), p. 35. While this book was written late in the progressive period, it reflects views consistently held much earlier by Bower and others. See Walter S. Athearn, "Protestantism and Democracy," in *Addresses and Proceedings of the Sixteenth Annual Meeting* (Boston: NEA, 1922); Shailer Mathews, *The Social Gospel*

(Philadelphia: Griffith & Rowland Press, 1910), pp. 140-43; Washington Gladden, "Religion and the Schools," *Atlantic Monthly* 115 (January 1915):57-68; William Clayton Bower, "Church as Educator," in *The Church at Work in the Modern World,* ed. William Clayton Bower (Chicago: University of Chicago Press, 1935), pp. 107-33.

10. Athearn, *Religious Education and American Democracy, p. 14. For complimentary views see Bower, "Church as Educator," pp. 110-19; George Albert Coe, "Our Two-Headed System of Education: The Problem Defined," Religious Education* 22 (June 1927):564-67; Henry F. Cope, *The Modern Sunday School in Principle and Practice,* 2nd ed. (New York: Fleming H. Revell Co., 1907), pp. 9-10.

11. William Clayton Bower, "Adjustment of the Church to a Changing Culture," *Religious Education* 25 (March 1930):217. Bower's analysis is quite interesting. He argued that the church substituted amelioration and busyness for real social reconstruction: "*Because* religion, in its uncritical acquiescence in the *status quo,* has to that extent lost its essential character *as religion,* it unconsciously seeks to escape from reality and to compensate for its incompetence by resorting to elaboration of the institution by erecting buildings, by the development of liturgy, and by excessive busy-ness about the issues that are irrelevant to the fundamental issues of a machine age" (p. 218). See also Shailer Mathews, "The Development of Social Christianity in America During the Past Twenty-five Years," *Journal of Religion* 7 (July 1927):376-86.

12. Arthur Cushman McGiffert, "A Teaching Church," *Religious Education* 16 (February 1921):5. See also Gladden, "Religion and the Schools," pp. 61-63.

13. Bower, "Adjustment of the Church," p. 219. See also George Albert Coe, "Religious Education and Political Conscience," *Teachers College Record* 23 (September 1922):297-304; idem, *What Is Christian Education?* (New York: Charles Scribner's Sons, 1930), pp. 13-19, 240-62; Athearn, "Protestantism and Democracy," pp. 519-21.

14. Henry F. Cope, "Twenty Years' Progress in Religious Education," *Religious Education* 18 (October 1923):314.

15. E.g., see Marianna C. Brown, *Sunday-School Movement in America* (New York: Fleming H. Revell Co., 1901); Henry F. Cope, *The Evolution of the Sunday School* (Boston: Pilgrim Press, 1911); idem, "Ten Years Progress in Religious Education," *Religious Education* 13 (June 1913):117-49. The first ten years' issues of *Religious Education,* as well as the proceedings of the official meetings of the International Sunday School Association (ISSA) and the Sunday School Council of Evangelical Denominations (SSCED) are also filled with these concerns during the second decade of the twentieth century.

16. See "Educational and Extension Section" in *Minutes, Sixth Annual Meeting* (Philadelphia: George T. Webb, Secretary, SSCED, 1916), pp. 39-57.

17. See particularly Walter S. Athearn, chr., "The Church School: Report of the Committee on the 'Correlation of Educational Agencies of the Local Church,' " *Religious Education* 8 (April 1913):32-47; Henry F. Cope, *Efficiency in the Sunday School* (New York: George N. Doran Co., 1912); Wilhelmina Stooker, "Sunday Sessions and Related Activities—Children's Work," in *Papers and Addresses Given at Eleventh Annual Meeting* (Toronto: Council Office, SSCED, 1921), pp. 61-64.

18. Athearn, "Church School: Reports of Committee," pp. 34-36. See also Walter Athearn, *The Church School* (Boston: Pilgrim Press, 1914).

19. E. B. Chappell, chr., "Report of Committee on Courses of Study for the Sunday School," in *Minutes, Fourth Annual Meeting* (Philadelphia: Office of the Secretary, SSCED, 1914), p. 55; *Organized Sunday School Work in North America, 1914–1918: Proceedings of Fifteen International Sunday School Convention* (Chicago: ISSA, 1918), pp. 94-99. A comprehensive description of models of weekday religious education can be found in "Committee on Religious Education and the Public Schools," in *Minutes, Seventh Annual Meeting* (Philadelphia: George T. Webb, Secretary, SSCED, 1917), pp. 56-62.

20. Athearn, *Religious Education and American Democracy,* p. 21; see also Walter S. Athearn, *Character Building in a Democracy* (Boston: Pilgrim Press, 1924).

21. Athearn, "Protestantism and Democracy," p. 521.

22. *Report of Committee on Education,* pp. 36-37.

23. Athearn, *Religious Education and American Democracy,* p. 2. For a program of community religious education, see *Papers and Addresses,* pp. 16-77, which includes articles on essential elements, organization, and implications for children, youth, and adults.

24. *Organized Sunday School Work 1914–1918,* p. 95.

25. William Clayton Bower, *The Educational Task of the Local Church* (St. Louis: Teacher Training Publishing Association, 1921), pp. 42-43. See also Henry F. Cope, *Religious Education in the Church* (New York: Charles Scribner's Sons, 1918), description of coordinating a church for a total ministry.

26. See, e.g., Frank Sheldon, "The Essential Elements in a Community Program of Religious Education," in *Papers and Addresses,* pp. 16-17.

27. Adelaide T. Case, "Christian Education," in *The Church Through Half a Century,* ed. Samuel McCrea Cavert and Henry Pitney Van Dusen (New York: Charles Scribner's Sons, 1936), pp. 229-47.

28. See, e.g., Henry F. Cope, *The Modern Sunday School and Its Present Day Task* (New York: Fleming H. Revell Co., 1907–1916), pp. 62-72; idem, *Education for Democracy,* p. 49; idem, "Twenty Years' Progress," p. 313; Athearn, "Protestantism's Contribution to Character Building," p. 28; Theodore G. Soares, "Religious Education," in *Religious Thought in the Last Quarter-Century,* ed. Gerald Birney Smith (Chicago: University of Chicago Press, 1927), pp. 167-84.

29. Washington Gladden, "The Dominant Function of the Church," *Religious Education* 8 (June 1913):150; Mathews, "Development of Social Christianity," p. 386; idem, "Let Religious Education Beware," *Christian Century* 44 (March 24, 1927):363-64.

30. For an analysis of the continuing effect of the domestication of churches' education, see Stephen A. Schmidt, *A History of the Religious Education Association* (Birmingham, Ala.: Religious Education Press, 1983).

31. For biographical material on the life of George Albert Coe, see the articles published in *Religious Education* at the time of his retirement in 1927 and his death in 1952: *Religious Education* 22 (January 1927):100; *Religious Education* 47 (March-April 1952):67-96. See also an analysis of Coe's life and influence in Jack L. Seymour, *From Sunday School to Church School* (Washington, D.C.: University Press, 1982), pp. 127-53.

32. Hartshorne, "George Albert Coe," *Religious Education* 22 (January 1927): 100.

33. George Albert Coe, "Religious Education as a Part of General Education," in *Who Are We? The Quest for a Religious Education,* ed. John Westerhoff, III (Birmingham: Religious Education Press, 1978), p. 20.

34. For biographical material on the life of William Clayton Bower, see William Clayton Bower, *Through the Years: Personal Memoirs* (Lexington: Transylvania College Press, 1957); Valarie Honeycutt, "Dr. William Bower, Educator and Theologian, Dies at 104," *Lexington Herald* (July 26, 1982).

35. Bower, *Through the Years,* pp. 77-93.

36. Ibid., p. 74.

37. George Albert Coe, "Burning Issues," *Religious Education* (Special Convention Issue, 1928):652.

38. Bower, "Facing the Future: The Church's Response to Social Change," in *Church at Work in the Modern World,* ed. Bower, pp. 279-85.

39. See, e.g., Bower, "Adjustment of the Church to a Changing Culture," pp. 217-19; idem, "Church as Educator," pp. 110-14; idem, "Possibilities and Dangers of Institutionalized Religion," in *Religion and Conduct,* ed. George H. Betts, Frederick C. Eiselen, and George Albert Coe (New York: Abingdon Press, 1930), pp. 108-10; George Albert Coe, "The Elusiveness of 'Religion'," *Religious Education* 31 (January 1936):43; idem, "Let Us Rethink the Purpose of Religious Education," *Religious Education* 23 (December 1928):974-78; idem, *What Is Religion Doing to Our Consciences?* (New York: Charles Scribner's Sons, 1943).

40. Coe, "Our Two Headed System of Education: The Problem Defined," *Religious Education* 22 (June 1927):568.

41. Coe, *What Is Christian Education?* p. 254.

42. William Clayton Bower, "Christian Education after Nineteen Centuries," *Religion in Life* 12 (Winter 1943-44):46.

43. For sources on their understanding of the function of religion in society, see Bower, "Making the Resources of Religion Available in Education,"

*Religious Education* 36 (January-March 1941):3-5; idem, "Adjustment of the Church to a Changing Culture," pp. 218-19; idem, *Church and State in Education*, pp. 41-56; George Albert Coe, "The Elusiveness of Religion," *Religious Education* 31 (January 1936):43-45; idem, "For Such a Time as This," *Religious Education* 37 (May-June 1942):132-37; idem, *What Is Christian Education?*; idem, "The Religious Outlook of the World Today," *Religious Education* 31 (April 1936):89-90.

44. George Albert Coe, *A Social Theory of Religious Education* (New York: Charles Scribner's Sons, 1927), p. 264.

45. George Albert Coe, "The Public Mind," in *Religion and Public Affairs*, ed. Harris Franklin Rall (New York: Macmillan Co., 1937), p. 204.

46. Coe, *What Is Christian Education?* p. 22.

47. Bower, "Making the Resources of Religion Available in Education," pp. 6-7.

48. Coe, "Public Mind," p. 209.

49. For a description, see, e.g., William Clayton Bower, *The Curriculum of Religious Education* (New York: Charles Scribner's Sons, 1925); George Albert Coe, "Emergent Democracy: 1932–1938," *School and Society* 47 (June 11, 1938):752-55.

50. Bower, *Church and State in Education*, pp. 58-59, 78 (quote, p. 57).

51. Idem, *Through the Years*, p. 73.

52. Idem, *Church and State in Education*, p. 94, italics added.

53. Coe, *Social Theory of Religious Education*, pp. 262-63. This conviction is also one reason both Coe and Bower, later in life, criticized church education influenced by neo-orthodox theology; they thought it limited religious education to the church and thus restricted the scope of the church's educational responsibilities. See Bower, *Through the Years*, pp. 59-60.

54. Coe, *What Is Christian Education?* pp. 30-34 (quote, p. 33).

55. William Clayton Bower, "A Curriculum for Character and Religious Education in a Changing Culture," *Religious Education* 25 (February 1930):130-33. Also see Coe, "What Education for Peace Could Accomplish: Unrealized Aims of Far-Reaching Importance," *International Journal of Religious Education* 14 (November 1937):8-9.

56. Paul Tillich, *Theology of Culture*, ed. Robert C. Kimball (Oxford: Oxford University Press, 1959), pp. 156-57.

# CHAPTER V

# The
# Religious
# in Education

THROUGHOUT the history of the United States, its people have continually been forced to redefine their life together and the shape of their culture—in other words, to redefine themselves as a public. National expansion, immigration, and the increasing complexity of economic life have repeatedly demanded new solutions to the problem of combining a respect for individual differences with the preservation of national unity. Usually these solutions have been rooted in Western definitions of the character of human life—rationality, technological efficiency, and the normativeness of "white" social patterns. Such principles have encouraged education and democracy, but they also have tended to accommodate diversity to a Western, Protestant paradigm of culture.

The present era represents another challenge to the comprehensiveness and inclusiveness of the United States public: The debates over the national role in "peacekeeping" around the world, the relationship of military expenditures to those for social services, and the inclusion of diverse ethnic groups in political leadership are illustrative. There are advocates of an intensified nationalism whose views of the public are defined by national boundaries and a narrow understanding of Jewish and Christian traditions. Their work is seen in many contemporary Christian day schools which attempt to educate their young people to maintain and extend that vision of a "Christian America" formulated in the mid-nineteenth century. There are also leaders in the so-called industrial-military complex who assume that the public transcends geographical and ideological boundaries and consists of those around the world with the resources to buy into their competitive values and goals. That still others are restive with these operational definitions of the public can be seen in struggles for racial, social, economic, and sexual inclusiveness, not only in the United States, but around the globe.

The rhetoric of the past is being tested. What does the promise in the Declaration of Independence regarding "life, liberty, and the pursuit of happiness" really mean today for those who lacked the franchise at the time those words were first written and have sought full inclusion ever since—the descendants of slaves and Native Americans, specifically, and women generally? What does that same promise mean in a nation with no new frontier out of which the poor and dispossessed might carve a future? What does the invitation of the European-oriented Statue of Liberty mean to the "poor and huddled masses" who pour into this country through Miami and the port cities of the West Coast, and across the Mexican border? The view of the public that has dominated the imagination of the citizens of the nation is being thoroughly challenged from many sides.

Within the churches, an ambivalence toward a redefinition of the public can also be seen. Some look for an extension of the nation's manifest destiny that will preserve patterns of "Protestant America." Others criticize prevailing public actions as limited nationalistic definitions of the worth of human beings. Their concerns are seen in recent movements for national nuclear, military, and economic responsibility.

Still others reflect identities and loyalties to a worldwide community which lead them to view nationalistic commitments as more like the loyalty of family members to a village society than a public infused with Christian concern for all God's children. The churches of the United States seem as confused as the people themselves about the appropriate shape of a public vision and how to effect it.

Our task in exploring the role of the churches in the formation and education of the public is made even more difficult by the lack of any clearly emerging strategy to delineate the role of the church in contemporary educational tasks of defining public life. The situation of those of us in the churches contrasts dramatically with that of our Puritan ancestors. Guided by a clear vision of the nature of the public as a people in covenant with God, they assumed that religion was its foundation and that the church, through education, would significantly shape and direct its life.

Our situation also differs significantly from that of the mid-nineteenth-century Protestant and Catholic leaders who sought to preserve their own definition of the public in the midst of increased immigration and industrial and urban change. While they developed specific educational strategies which persist even to this day, those strategies, as we have seen, tended to leave the churches with the primary domestic task of incorporating persons into their own life, rather than working at the continual task of the construction of the public. The liberal religious educators of the early twentieth century, increasingly aware of this diminished role, sought to reclaim for the church a more broadly defined function in the development of a public identity and consciousness by linking church school education to public school education. But they still assumed the continuing unfolding of a Christian society, bounded by the ideology and geography of the nation. It is our belief that today such a perspective is both parochial and illusory.

Hence our task is different from that of our forebears. We are confronted with the necessity of participating in a quest for a definition of the public and, at the same time, clarifying for the church its distinctive function and its contribution to the formation of a more inclusive public identity. We have no clear program to offer the church and its educational ministry in this time. Clear programs and strategies result in times when definitions and goals themselves are clear. Nevertheless, it is our conviction that churches have a critically significant role to play in the very formation of those definitions and goals. But unless we are careful, the present domestication of the church will exclude it from conversations about national goals and paideia. Therefore we will suggest several clues to assist churches' recognition of their task, which fundamentally is one of reclaiming the religious in education. By "the religious," we mean the discernment and mediation of the sacred dimensions of reality.[1] Our contention is that the transcendent is present in human life and that its mediation pushes us beyond everyday, typical understandings of reality, to open up new possibilities for human life and organization. Too often the churches miss the power of the transcendent to shape public life because they themselves are captured by the everyday. They must reconnect themselves to those transcendent sources and infuse conversation about the public with that power and those possibilities.

## The Necessity of the Religious in the Public

The previous chapters have told the story of the continual domestication of the churches' education—that their contribution has been circumscribed into a task of gathering members and providing personal meanings for those members to help them tolerate the ambiguities of public life. The result has been a religious void in the public itself so pervasive that, in spite of the popularity of church attendance, we can characterize the present public as almost religionless.

This situation is most clearly apparent in sociological and anthropological studies of the relation of church to culture. The experience of one typical small town in the Midwest may be paradigmatic. Mapletown is the classic reflection of the "American" dream of opportunity, prosperity, and comfort, where individuals can pursue their own ends amidst a supportive community.[2] Incorporated in 1859, its history reflects the pioneering spirit of the nation's people, determined to build a civilization out of the forests and wilderness. While its economy still revolves primarily around agriculture, Mapletown has a growing industrial base, an excellent school system with colleges nearby, and the shopping, services, and medical facilities necessary for a comfortable life.

Over the past twenty years, two international anthropologists, one from France and the other from India, have analyzed the role of religion in the social structure of Mapletown. Their conclusions reveal the dilemma of a religionless public. On the surface, the church seemed to have a central place in the life of the town. For example, each Friday the local newspaper published a full-page advertisement sponsored by local businesses, listing the services of all the churches—Catholic, mainline Protestant, and fundamentalist. It even emphasized the felt intrinsic relationship of the church to the community in its lead statement: "The Church is the greatest faith on earth for the building of character and good citizenship. It is a storehouse of spiritual values. Without a strong Church, neither democracy nor civilization can survive."[3] On the surface, then, the church seemed central. Church membership was valued, and public civic rituals demanded prayer and the presence of a church leader.

Yet on a deeper level, both anthropologists discovered that the church had little influence on the activity of the people in their civic life. One anthropologist commented that "democracy," rather than religion, was the foundation for most people's values; the other concluded, "Religious upbringing does not directly *cause* any major deflection from the common American cause."[4] The churches therefore acted as a support for the "American paideia" of the community rather than being an actual influence in the continual shaping of the paideia.

The churches seemed important only because they fit within the voluntary pattern of the United States social structure. As voluntary associations alongside other voluntary associations, the churches existed because they met the personal needs of members and provided a community of personal support within which to grow and to feel comfortable in the ambiguities of public life. The people of the town loved the churches because there they could experience a rewarding fellowship with others, express personal and aesthetic differences, have marriages sanctified and children baptized and educated, and be supported in times of sickness, crisis, and death. Yet paradoxically, these same members could not explain how the churches actually affected their lives in the public sphere.[5] The church, it seems, had become so intimate a part of the social structure that it replicated the values of the society, rather than providing a means to connect life to the sacred. Its social function, then, was to integrate individuals into cultural patterns, rather than to affect those patterns.

The ritual, symbolic, and educational life of the churches was clearly domesticated. The churches expended their energy on differentiating themselves from other church groups, so their educational systems were designed to attract members and reinforce their participation. The result of this domestication was that the churches neither directly shaped public life nor probed the depth of religious reality for living. Even the symbols of the churches seemed to lose a sacred dimension.[6] Therefore the sacred, or religious, dimension of reality was made known to neither the church members nor the public itself. Church life was "business as usual," merely paralleling and reinforcing the patterns of the community social structure. It is therefore not surprising that people could not express the way church discourse should affect their living in the public, for it had lost a religious dimension.[7] And thus the community itself became a public devoid of the religious.

The result of a religious void in the public, or a religionless public, is the closing off of the gracious possibilities in human social life which transcend mundane daily living. Life, thought, and human organization are then limited to and controlled by everyday definitions of reality. Living is business as usual. The transcendent dimensions are lost.

This avoidance of the transcendent is seen in conversations about the role of religion in education in the United States. As education became increasingly secularized, many educators claimed that the exclusion of the study of religion would subvert morality and the formation of values.[8] They tended to understand religion only instrumentally: It functioned to provide morality. Religion then was reduced to another element in the modern Western perspective—a perspective concerned with defining practical reality, controlling reality through technological efficiency, and predicting the outcome of actions.

This modern world-view is exclusively occupied with the everyday, that which can be touched, manipulated, and rationally analyzed. To oversimplify, this world-view equals what has been called the pragmatism of the United States. Such a pragmatism has resulted in scientific and technological advancement, efficient forms of organization, and the manufacture of a plethora of products to make everyday living easier. We can produce incredible nuclear power to generate electricity for millions, but this power also can destroy the world. We can expand medical technology to cure many of the ill, but we so increase the cost of care that it loses general availability unless there is significant government intervention. The mind-set of the everyday is concerned with control, power, and manipulation.

Many have written about the practical and philosophical results of this concern with the everyday.[9] Their arguments can be summarized in what Peter Berger terms the *Homeless Mind*.[10] The mind can solve technical problems of production and control, but it cannot give us the meanings for understanding our own powers. Or, as we have noted, a human gap develops between growing technological complexity and our capacity to cope with that complexity.[11] We are terrorized by our own pragmatic human creations.[12]

While any world-view provides meanings, we are no longer capable of living with a world-view devoted only to everyday meanings of control and production. We are in need of religious meanings which provide new ways of understanding the process of world creation itself. The religious dimension of reality has too long been ignored in the concentration on the everyday. The religious confronts human understanding and will—in terms of eternity, in terms of the ultimate, in terms of creativity itself.

The distinguished historian of religions Huston Smith has carefully articulated the result of an exclusive focus on the everyday:

> The triumphs of modern science—all in the material world, remember—have swung our attention toward the world's material aspects. The consequence—could anything be more natural?—has been progressive inattention to certain of the world's other properties. Stop attending to something and first we forget its importance; from there it is only a matter of time till one begins to wonder if it exists at all.[13]

He continues: The modern Western mind-set "that aims relentlessly at control rules out the possibility of transcendence in principle."[14] Therefore the human gap results—a homelessness of addressing and responding to everyday meanings.

This consequence is precisely what one of the anthropologists discovered in Mapletown: The activities of the churches camouflaged a deeper and "growing spiritual vacuum on account of lack of faith."[15] He implies that a focus on the sacred and religious dimensions of reality that birthed the church is itself an essential task of the church as an influence in public life—as the leaven in society.

Here, we believe, is the mandate for the education of the church: It must reclaim its religious task, what Huston Smith calls the Sacred Unconscious, "that luminous mystery in which all things are bathed."[16] While the sacred can never be controlled by our minds or our actions and is revealed to us only as "a fleeting glimpse of possibility," it is this dimension beyond the everyday that discloses meaning, hope, grace, and creativity.[17] The church's task consists of much more than the efficient teaching of the content and practices of a religion, as many progressive educators had thought—it is concerned rather with the mediation of the religious dimension to reality.

Many have explored and defined the religious dimension of life in its complexity.[18] In this study, though, it is enough to say that religious processes are simply defined as the openness of human beings to transcendence. To live life religiously is to live *sub specie aeternitatis* (in light of eternity). Human beings live in a context simultaneously everyday and transcendent. Therefore religions are human attempts to embody the religious in concrete history. The fundamental question is: How can we be human in light of eternity and the sacred?[19] People do experience depth and grace and possibility in their lives. Religions, through their stories, images, and symbols, have historically pointed to and mediated this depth, a religious reality. The Christian religion, as one religious community, must recognize its responsibility for the mediation of transcendence. This is its educational task in the construction of the public.

Each faith community provides its members with stories and a tradition to tell how God has acted in history and to clarify the vision for history itself. They also provide a present experience of people struggling together to be faithful to the presence of God in human experience. The variety of faith communities and the diversity of their meanings portray clearly the complexity and depth of the attempt to respond to the presence of the sacred in the world—a presence fundamentally concerned with the character of human life and organizations.

It is imperative that churches, as mediators of the religious, teach their multiple traditions, for these provide ways by which persons throughout time have sought to respond to ultimate meaning in daily experiences. Moreover, these churches also provide processes through which persons understand and engage the religious dimension in human life in communities in the present.

Here is the context for constructive reflection on the task of religious education. The church, which helped to form the character of this nation, accomplished its task so well that today it has a clear role to play within the total educational ecology. Yet through this role, the church has become subservient to the culture's definition of itself. The church now replicates the United States social structure. If its education is to be more than domesticated in the system, the church must first refocus education on the religious dimension and then recognize and engage the role it plays in the education of the public.

### Toward a Religious Approach for Church Education

Society in the United States is characterized by an incredibly intricate network of production and distribution, transportation, communication, government and legal systems, with rationality in the pursuit of its goals as its hallmark. The spirit of efficient bureaucracy, as embodied in rational planning, role hierarchies, and discipline in the pursuit of goals, pervades every aspect of our lives. Max Weber's haunting image describes what our existence is becoming: an iron cage, in which rational or bureaucratic social organization gradually crushes our capacity to be attuned to the magic and mystery of our world. "The ultimate and most sublime values have retreated from public life either into the transcendental realm of mystic life or into the brotherliness of direct and personal human relations [the domesticated private realm]."[20]

As people living in this culture, we experience life as means-oriented, to be used, changed, solved, and had. It is this disposition that must be transformed if religious meanings are ever to break into our daily life in a way that will affect the public world. But the tide of everyday living in our nation's form of society shapes all our experience in precisely the opposite direction.

Edward Robinson of Manchester College at Oxford reminds us that the imagination of a people is stunted by the influence of an acquisitive, competitive, materialistic society (and, it can be added, by the kind of education such a society attempts to instill to perpetuate its values). Such stunting blocks a culture's spiritual potential and creates a religionless public.[21] We as church educators must respond to this void. We believe this public need may be addressed if we can fashion an education that will focus on imagination as it relates to sacrament in the faith community.

An education that aims to provide the public with a religious meaning where such has been eclipsed needs to address that certain power of imagination that is capable of self and society re-creation. It is only when our self images and social images are re-formed that we then change our beliefs, values, and judgments about the meaning of our life together, our public being, and thus change our actions.

Our concern is to educate for a religious imagination. *Religious* means experiencing the holy as present in concrete historical life. For Christians, the religious imagination is a "sacramental" imagination, one that sees all reality in terms of the presence of God in Jesus Christ.

Therefore an exploration of the sacramental imagination provides a direction for the kind of education that is needed in our day. In our world, the task of the churches' education is to infuse the public imagination with the religious.

As we have established, the problem has been that the meanings of both education and religion have been restricted. We have ignored a subtle but profound transformation from religious to secular, in public life, language, and meaning, allowing only a small role for religion and eclipsing its power to focus us on the transcendent. Further, we have redirected education from a focus on images that make meaning of our experience to a concentration on beliefs that lead us to a privatized caretaking rather than to public outreach.

Andrew Greeley has provided clarification of religion and its connection to education:

> Religion is first of all, experience, an experience of the holy, the sacred, the good, and then it's image and the memory which recalls that experience, what we would call a symbol, and then, it's the story we tell to others to explain the symbol and to recount our experience. That's religion. We go beyond that and reflect. We create catechisms and theologies, but the basic raw power comes from the experience, the image and the story.[22]

Most of us, however, are unaware of the images that focus our lives, and even of the source for those images. But it is the images, along with the symbols, rituals, language, and narratives of our culture that are our primary educators.

Imagination, then, is at the heart of education. Education

begins at the moment we draw upon our images, or pictures, to focus the experiences our human sensitivities and sensibilities encounter in the world. As Greeley states, "The experience [of the holy] is recorded first of all in that aspect of the personality we normally call 'the imagination.'" Our senses are impacted by an experience, which is then filtered through the imagination. The interaction between experience and imagination is complex and intricate. A given person or community responds to an experience with the images and pictures that are available in the imagination, and this response shapes the perception of the experience and its later recollection. Thus it can be said that the imagination shapes the experience.[23]

This encounter, then, is a mutual action of two agents: Our experience of the world acts upon us, and we, by imagining that experience, act upon the world. An even closer look reveals that the imagination frames the picture we take of our experience of the world. The power of the imagination is in its forming of the reality we experience. To repeat: Our imagination takes what we sense and shapes it, giving it form and content.

According to Greeley, the imagination provides the symbols, which resonate with the reality that has been experienced. Religion, then, infuses the imagination with a sacred dimension. The power of religious language stirs up resonances of experience similar to the experience of the religious storyteller.

The telling each year [during] Holy Week of the story of the death and resurrection of Jesus, complete with all the profoundly resonating liturgical imagery is . . . designed . . . to rekindle memories of death-rebirth experiences that have marked the lives of the hearers and to link those resonances to the historic experience of Christians through the ages, leading back to the founding experience itself. The Easter story, in other words, is primarily designed to rekindle memories of grace experiences and link them with overarching memories in the historical tradition. Religion as story leaps from imagination.[24]

Religion, then, is meaning-seeking behavior. Meaning is encoded in symbols, whose power is accounted for by

rooting them in experiences of grace which renew human hopefulness in a given individual biography. A person undoubtedly approaches such experiences, at least in his adult life, with a repertory of pictures and stories which he has inherited from his religious tradition, so that in adult life and perhaps even childhood (though not, perhaps, in early childhood) the propositions may chronologically precede experience and symbol. But the driving force of religion, I contend, is experiential, imaginative, symbolical, and narrational, not propositional; and, I submit, perhaps the fundamental testable proposition in my theory is that it is the religious imagination which will predict behavior, not religious propositions.[25]

According to this perspective, we can see that in previous eras of Christian education, we were dealing with religion thrice removed from experience—after story and after symbol. We were concerned with the propositions of catechism and theologies and rote behaviors.

Our imagination precedes the words, or names, we give to what we sense. It precedes the judgments we make, the values we hold, the beliefs we formulate, and the actions we take. Thus imagination is crucial to education; it is where we must begin to reshape our self-image and our public environment.[26]

Imagination is fundamentally an expression of our world-view. That is, behind imagination, behind knowing, behind naming, behind education, is faith. In other words, our imagination does its work on the basis of faith. As Christians, our faith, or the world-view that informs reality for us, is the mystery of the incarnation, the Word of God made flesh. This means that our very image of the world and all we experience is shaped by the notion that the world (the flesh) is capable of being God-filled. The world, then, for Christians, is "sacramental"—capable of being God-filled. All reality, by analogy to the incarnation of God in Jesus Christ, can be seen by Christians as having the potential for the God/human relationship found in Jesus Christ. All reality is imagined as capable of being enfleshed by God, analogous of the way God is enfleshed in Jesus Christ.

Understanding sacrament as our way of participating in the incarnate presence of God (that is, making the world holy), we can now use that term to describe, or name, the shape of the frame (faith) of Christians' imagination. It is a sacramental imagination. This means that when Christians encounter the world, they do so with an imagination framed so as to see all reality in terms of God's incarnate presence.

A sacramental imagination is drawn from the stories of the community of faith, the church. The way we perceive reality, the way we name it and respond to it, is given to us by our community. From the stories of the community, we receive our incarnational view of life. Story is the response people make to mystery. Story is the creation of worlds in which people live, move, and act. As we grapple with the experience of mystery (the Holy, the Ultimate), we seek to make sense of the experience so that we can order, arrange, value, choose, symbolize, and express. While one can certainly tell one's own story, it is more important to recognize that stories are primarily the domain of communities and that one's own life (or story) is shaped in interaction with the stories of one's community.

Christians describe the church not only as the community that gives the stories that fire our sacramental imagination, but as a sacrament itself. It is the living, historical extension of Jesus Christ. The church itself is an instrument by which God's grace is accomplished. The church, then, like Jesus Christ, is both a sign of union with God and an instrument to achieve this union and unity. Just as Jesus Christ served God as a living instrument of salvation, so, in a similar way, Christ is served by the church.

As can be seen by examining the two elements of our approach, imagination and faith community, the church is the place for both shaping the imagination and exercising it. Both the shaping and the exercising are the educational tasks of the church. We have already seen what it means to shape a sacramental imagination; now it is necessary to look at what it means to exercise sacramental imagination.

For the Christian all reality is seen as potential sacrament of God. This means all reality is open to *transformation*. While the sacraments such as baptism and the Eucharist are surely acts of God and Christ, they are mediated by the church. They are expressions of its very nature and mission, moments that recall a past, effect a present, and signify or point to a future. These sacraments, celebrated in and by the community of faith, both inform the recipients' world-views and call them to create environments in which the gospel's view of peace and justice and love is affirmed, expressed, and lived. The traditional definition of sacrament is *Sacramenta efficiunt quod significant et significant quod efficiunt* (sacraments both point to what they cause and cause what they point to). *To sacrament*, then, is ultimately *to transform, to do justice*.

> The sacramental imagination both creates ritual contexts within which justice is done so as to nourish our quest for justice as well as fire our moral imagination as we critically try to discern what sacrament implies for, and moves us to do in society.[27]

The sacraments, for the Christian, contribute to the understanding of the general outline of the way life is to be lived, the way society is to be structured. A guiding biblical image for the mission of Christians is the kingdom of God. When we speak of the kingdom of God, we are talking about ways of living together, both in religious community and in the public community. We are also talking about the way God is transforming human life. Sacrament is the celebration of the growing presence of the spirit of God in the world. Sacraments call for ways of dwelling in religious community and the public world. They give Christians a general outline of the way to live, as well as suggest the need to structure environments for the coming of the Kingdom. For example, baptism nurtures the Christian in a new birth, or conversion and transformation, and so calls on him or her to structure the environment so that openness to change and conversion is valued. Eucharist disposes a person to thankfulness for God's gifts, expresses unity in communion, and thereby calls for an environment of unity and fellowship. This sacrament is both a personal response of gratitude for being made whole and a call for a social environment of peace (shalom) and harmony.[28]

Thus an education that focuses on sacramental imagination produces a community of faith which "sacraments"— that is, does justice. Educationally, the church does justice by addressing the world's images, infusing the world's imagination.

A religious approach is present in church education when sacramental imagination is its focus. Here is one coin with two sides. On one side, the self and the community are shaped by the image of Christ; on the other side, the environment is reshaped by the direct (educational) presentation of images which infuse society and provide the meaning for persons to act for justice.

Thus in summary, a religious approach to education in the church is based upon the belief that we are created in the image and likeness of God—that is, through the redemption effected in Jesus Christ, we are called to be co-creators. It is through our imagination that we co-create. We name the animals and infuse society with holy (religious) images. The true fruitfulness of our imagination is attained when we

141

reshape (re-create) both ourselves and our environment, to the mutual enrichment of both. Our task is a corporate one, done as a church, a people in a community of faith. In the church we gather the resources of our history—our stories of the way God acts in our lives, the wonderful things God has done to us, in us, for us, through us, and with us through Christ. It is as a church, a people of a faith community, that we enact these stories through our participation in sacramental (God present) rites, which shape us, and through which we reshape our environment to one of peace and justice. The religious approach to education described here calls us to the dual task of shaping and exercising our sacramental imagination.

## Toward a Strategy for the Church in the Education of the Public

If the church were committed to the tasks of shaping and exercising the imagination, its education would be quite different from one with an emphasis upon recruiting and training members. While these institutional goals are important, our alternative transcends their tendency toward domestication by stressing the conscious involvement of the church at the intersection of religious and cultural images in the formation of both personal and cultural life. It would become a means for infusing the symbols of transcendence into our reflections on the meanings of the political, social, and economic events of daily living. It would shift the educational tasks of the church from supporting and sustaining the private spheres of congregational life, to shaping the life and work of the congregation so that it might serve as an agent of transcendence in the public.

A new strategy is needed for the church's participation in the formation of the emerging paideia. Here we suggest five clues to guide church educators in that task. The first has to do with recognizing and reclaiming the role of the church in the emerging educational ecology. The second and third are clues to shaping in persons the sacramental imagination which provides the distinctive contribution of the church in the education of the public. And the last two are clues to the exercise of an imaginative posture in the public, which undergirds the transformatory function of the church in public life.

*First, church education must recognize and claim its formative role in the education of the public.* Martin Marty points to this clue when he observes that the public church, as the "family of apostolic churches with Jesus Christ at the center," and with special sensitivity to the "res publica," does not "await invention but discovery."[29] Simply the fact that churches are deeply involved in activities designed to influence the visions, values, and actions of people who live in the realm of public life illustrates their public character. But an education that takes seriously the task of helping to shape the public imagination does not concentrate its energies and resources upon the recruitment or training of people to be *in* the church. Its emphasis is upon *being* the church in the world. This is certainly not a new idea. The gospel called the early church to be *in* but not *of* the world. The history of the church illustrates the constant temptation of churches either to turn in upon themselves or to become reflections of the world. In either case, their contribution to the common life became irrelevant to the agenda of the public. The liberation churches of Latin America once again remind us that the church, when responding as the people of God, is "incarnated in the world, but not swallowed up by it. It expresses itself through the language and symbols of the people, but its message revolutionizes the meaning of both the language and symbols."[30] Virgilio Elizondo's point is that if we do not infuse the language and symbols of the everyday with the content of mystery and transcendence, we eliminate the religious from the domain of public discourse and perpetuate the dichotomy of religion and the public. The consequence is the privatization of religious experience and the domestication of the church's public role.

To *be* the church is a public posture. It projects congregations into the educational ecology of a community or culture as one of its formative agencies. The intentional action of *being* in the public acknowledges that the church must claim its responsibility for gathering people into and shaping the common life of both nation and global community. When churches assume a public posture, they are able to engage in the competitive and cooperative interaction of other agencies that are actively engaged in activities to influence the character and destiny both of individual people and of their common life.

As we noted in chapter 1, some educators believe that the task is of special significance now. Herman Niebuhr argues that the predominant educational ecology of the past several decades is shifting. New technologies, new patterns of work, increasing population diversity, and changing views of authority have effectively challenged the functional effectiveness of the network of schools, churches, families, and other informal educational agencies. The newly emerging "learning system," as Niebuhr calls it, requires a new kind of consciousness of the contribution and relationship of each agency to the whole.[31]

The church cannot assume that a place will be made for it in this newly emerging ecology. It is the church that must intentionally engage in contemporary conversations regarding the future of our public life and claim its place as one of the primary mediating structures for making meaningful connections between personal life and public policy.

In that role, the church can help to sanction personal values and meanings and enrich the public realm with its images, stories, and symbols. It can participate in the educational ecology of the nation as the agency of mystery and transcendence, infusing the whole of our common life with a religious dimension. Hence the task of church education must necessarily engage in those actions that shape and exercise what we have called a public and sacramental imagination.

*Second, to shape a sacramental imagination, church education must explore the function of religious experience in forming the faith of both individuals and communities.* Religious experience involves both the personal and the corporate encounters of people with the mystery beyond the boundaries of rational experience, that dimension of reality which transcends human comprehension yet intrudes into the midst of everyday life. Every faith community has its paradigmatic encounters with the holy. In the Jewish and Christian traditions: Moses' confrontation with "I am who I am" through the burning bush, Isaiah's vision in the temple; and for Christians, Saul's encounter with the risen Christ on the road to Damascus—these have been dramatic models of intrusion of the holy into the midst of everyday life. Quieter examples are still more common and illustrate the availability of the encounter to any who have "the eyes to see and the ears to hear": the woman with the hemmorrhage who simply sought to touch the hem of Jesus' robe; John Wesley's heightened hearing of Paul's words to the Romans; the wide-eyed wonder of a three-year-old who *sees* the baby Jesus in a live Christmas crèche.

The emphasis upon personal religious experience in contemporary United States piety means that many are not aware of the transforming power of corporate encounters with the holy. Pentecost is, for Christians, the paradigmatic illustration of the shared recognition of holy presence. For Jews, the Exodus may well be such a paradigmatic illustration. For contemporary citizens of the United States, recent corporate encounters with the holy may have occurred during the march on Washington at the height of the civil rights movement, the televised broadcasts of the funerals of John F. Kennedy and Martin Luther King, or the dedicatory service of the memorial to the soldiers who died in Vietnam. Those events were deeply imprinted on the corporate imagination of United States citizens and many others around the world. Their power is rooted in the shared experience of holy encounters.

Religious experience is the primal encounter of faith. As such it enlivens the imagination, challenges the ordinary and mundane, and calls into question the wisdom of the status quo. Imagination becomes the lens through which the routines and relationships of life are viewed and assessed, and provides the substance for reflective experience. Visions, stories, and rituals flow from the imagination and become the mediators of religious experience. Theology follows, as the interpretation of religious experience for public consciousness.

Church education cannot create or cause religious experience, though educators, like preachers and evangelists, have attempted to do so. The task of church education in shaping a sacramental imagination is rather to present the symbolic reality of the faith community's religious experience. It makes accessible to persons of all ages the symbols of a faith community's collective memory of its formative religious experiences. Couched in stories, images, and rituals, these symbols function as the connecting point between the mundane and transcendent dimensions of our existence. Charles Winquist has made the same point in his observation that symbols give expression "to the otherwise inexpressible union of conditional existence and unconditional reality."[32]

Stories, images, and rituals thereby become the basic content of church education. They provide models for behavior. They illuminate possibilities for meaning in life. Each of them becomes what Winquist has called an "integrating structure" which "organizes our feelings and forms a sense of continuous identity." Without them we become "disconnected from our past and future." We lose "our grip on the reality of our own identity with the passage of discrete moments." They provide, in other words, the possibility for meaning in the void that occurs between the visible displays of time on a digital watch. They enable us to acknowledge our relationship to both primordial and eschatological time and, above all, to see beyond the crisis of the immediate moment.[33] It is in the presentation of the stories, images, and rituals of a faith community's enlivened memories of its formative encounters with the holy that people obtain the resources for discerning—for "seeing and hearing"—the intersection of the holy and the mundane through the context of that faith community.

*Third, to shape a sacramental imagination, church education must develop methods for people to make meaning out of the interplay between their religious experience and their daily lives.* Theologians and Bible scholars are among the academicians who have recently discovered the potency of method in structuring and making sense of the object of their studies. Much of that interest has grown out of the recognition of the inadequacy of older methods. The situation is not unlike that which confronted the scientists of the eighteenth and nineteenth centuries following Newton's description of mechanistic theories for understanding the structure and relationship of the universe; or twentieth-century scientists, following Einstein's analysis of the relativity of matter. Among others, James Smart, Walter Brueggemann, James Sanders, and Daniel Patte have, in recent years, discussed the inadequacy of traditional methods of biblical scholarship for making sense out of the relationship between biblical and contemporary experience.[34] Similarly, David Tracy has observed that the theologian can no longer find in "the model for rational reflection developed by the Age of Enlightenment" an adequate way to articulate faith in a world marked by the "struggle to transcend our present individual and societal states in favor of a continuous examination of those illusions which cloud our real and more limited possibilities for knowledge and action."[35] Perhaps at no point is the bankruptcy of method more evident than in church members' prevailing tendency uncritically to apply biblical knowledge and theological categories to behavior. This rational and prescriptive mode of reflection has dominated popular Christian thought in the United States for decades. It was refined by the "lesson" that concluded each session of most Sunday school curriculum resources until fairly recently, reinforced by the "moral" that brought to climax the retelling of all too many Bible stories, and elevated into departments of "applied" theology in seminaries. The rationality, optimism, and simplicity of this method is simply no longer equal to the task of connecting the symbols of our religious experience to the nonrational dimensions of contemporary life. We can no longer assume the continuity of meanings through time, nor can we afford to reduce the educational role of the church to the development of moral character.

*Method,* as we are using the word, is more than technique. It is a mode of reflection through which people make meaning out of the connections between the mundane and transcendent dimensions of reality in their own experience. The primal content for these reflective modes of activity are the images, stories, and rituals that convey the symbols of religious experience through time and space to other people. But method moves a step beyond image, story, and ritual. The function of method is to form the structures for the imaginative apprehension and use of religious experience. It helps us to make sense, or meaning, out of those experiences for our daily lives and to engage in actions that are congruent with the intent of those meanings. Method, in this sense, becomes the occasion for movement into the future. Because it is a shared activity, it is also the source of disciplined reflective action in the life of the community of faith. It is the means by which people experience liberation, are transformed, or enabled to transcend the humdrum of the everyday.

There are at least four methods of reflection that educators and theologians must develop during the next few years. They are crucial to any Christian community seeking to contribute religious meanings to discussions on public life and policy: (1) methods that illuminate meanings from the Scriptures for our life and time; (2) methods for interpreting the symbolic linking of the holy with the everyday; (3) methods for interpreting contemporary experience out of the context of the history of the faith community's religious experience; and (4) methods for embodying those meanings for actions of justice in the world.

*Fourth, to exercise a sacramental imagination, church education needs to influence the processes for planning and implementing congregational ministries.* Here we are suggesting a stance contrary to popular practice in the administrative and management programming of the church. According to James D. Whitehead and Evelyn Eaton Whitehead, the skills associated with these two fields have been interpreted merely as borrowed techniques. They have not been translated into ministry skills with religious and theological content.[36] The consequence is evident in the extensive involvement of church educators in the training of persons in the goal setting and action phases of decision making, but often with little connection to the Christian stories, images, and rituals that could infuse their plans with the corporate traditions of religious experience. Similarly, in some denominations professional church educators have been given new responsibilities as program directors. This new office, however, has emphasized the management of the program life of a congregation, rather than exercising the religious imagination in planning and developing congregational ministries. This divorce of the religious from the decision-making processes only exacerbates the domestication we have described in the preceding chapters. It limits the exercise of the sacramental imagination to the realm of personal religious experience, denying, in the process, its public function—to shape the living of the congregation in the world.

A primary context for the exercise of the sacramental imagination is the congregation-in-ministry, which, from goal setting to action, infuses the planning process with the content of faith. It is rooted in religious experience and is evaluated by reflecting on whether a ministry event has been faithful to the formative religious experiences of the faith community.

The Whiteheads propose an educational model for the exercise of the sacramental imagination in the context of ministry—a model that moves in the direction toward which we are pointing. They describe one step as "attending to the faith of the community." This "involves discerning religious information as it arises in personal experience, in the community, and in the culture, as well as in the explicit formulation of Christian Tradition."[37] For the congregation this step entails clarifying the vision for its ministries. Grounded in the traditions of the community's collective religious experience and in its reading of the world, this vision becomes the basis for the selection of specific goals. The ultimate question facing a congregation as it plans into the future has to do with its faithfulness to (not its replication of) the meanings that have shaped its past. That faithfulness may be located both in the statements a congregation chooses to guide its ministries and in the manner in which it selects those goals and the procedures to implement them.

Every decision, in other words, is the occasion for religious reflection and ethical judgment. For example, does the life of a committee incarnate the meanings integral to the symbolic reality it seeks to embody? Is there congruence between the

150

faith commitments of committee members, their treatment of one another, and the motivations and procedures that shape their decisions and actions? At this point the Whiteheads' language provides another clue to the exercise of a sacramental imagination. It involves the assertion of one's personal and corporate religious convictions in the community. It moves ministry beyond the tasks of maintaining or expanding congregational life. Even those important decisions related to the ongoing internal program of a congregation are seen as the occasion for *being* the church rather than being *in* the church. It declares the public presence of the church in the midst of the ambiguity, confusion, tension, and illusions of contemporary life. It affirms the historic tradition of the church to witness to the power of the religious in life in the public. We are suggesting, in other words, that while the context for church education may include the school of a congregation in one of its several forms in shaping and exercising the sacramental imagination, it is also to be found in those places where the community of faith's decisions for ministry are explored, made, implemented, and celebrated.

*Fifth, to exercise a sacramental imagination, church education also needs to make connections with other public-minded agencies of the community, which, in spite of their potential differences, share a common commitment to shape the emerging paideia or vision of the common life.* Mid-nineteenth-century Protestant church leaders like Horace Bushnell recognized that churches could no longer function as the foundation of a society in the way our Puritan ancestors intended. But, with their Catholic colleagues, they still viewed the contribution of the church to be prescriptive. They supposed that the nation's culture would be inherently Christian and that the church's role was to create Christian citizens. In our own situation, the growing diversity of national life and the recognition that the public is not limited by national boundaries leads us to suggest another perspective for the contribution of the education of the church. This perspective takes an even more radical voluntary view of the composition of the ecology of educational agencies in the public. We can no longer assume that the church will participate in that ecology. We have seen all too clearly in the recent past how effectively churches have abdicated their public educational role while holding on to the rhetoric of public responsibility.

Instead, churches must begin to recognize the dynamic character of any contemporary educational ecology. They will participate in and contribute to that cooperative pattern of public formation insofar as they intentionally choose to assume a public role and support the other agencies of the community that share a common vision of the future of our common life. Church educators would then focus part of their attention upon mobilizing networks of community agencies, with the intention of negotiating educational programs and strategies for incorporating successive generations into the visions, attitudes, and values of the emerging paideia.

The role of church education in that ecology would be distinctive. It would center on infusing the life of the community with the religious. As stated earlier, this sacramental task involves embodying and transmitting the symbolic reality which illuminates the everyday with the mystery of transcendence. It means interpreting the stories, images, and rituals for the new time and place in which we find ourselves. For example, the religious significance of the Exodus was heightened for the Jews in Babylon. What does the story of that same formative religious experience mean to people around the world whose sacred lands face the threat of total destruction? Is there a place for us in the future? This is not a new question, but our response to it reveals the extent of our continuing involvement in that seminal religious experience.

152

Church education would also shift its emphasis away from prescribing moral responses for the guidance of personal and social behavior; such a perspective does not recognize the pluralistic character of our society, nor does it undergird the function of the religious in society. Instead, the education of the church would emphasize the ethical demands for justice and mercy that occur when the most noble of our thoughts and actions are revealed to be limited and self-serving in any encounter with the holy. In this sense church education is concerned with the prophetic task of illuminating public issues and decisions with transcendent meanings. It involves the development of understandings and skills for perceiving those human activities that are in harmony with God's intent for creation, and for calling into question those that thwart justice.

The church is in the public. Its presence cannot be ignored or dismissed. But its current tendency to focus its energies upon itself could all too easily diminish its contribution to the continuing task of forming public life. Faith communities, including Christian churches, are the primary agencies for the mediation of a religious perspective on all matters affecting our personal and corporate welfare. That contribution is dependent upon the presence in the public of a people whose visions, meanings, and skills have been given content and refined by participation in faith communities that seek to be responsive both to their heritage and to the agenda of the world.

We have attempted to explore the dangers of a church education that turns the church in upon itself. We have identified clues by which we believe the church may reclaim its religious role in public life. We extend an invitation to join us in the continuing venture to shape the church's education for this public role and responsibility.

## Notes

1. Throughout this study we have used the word *religious* as it is used in contemporary literature in the history of religions. *Religious* is therefore not an adjective, but a noun pointing to the depth and transcendent dimension of human social experience, that dimension of reality we call *the sacred.*

2. The data on Mapletown is drawn from two anthropological studies: Surajit Sinha, "Religion in an Affluent Society," *Current Anthropology* 7 (April 1966):189-94; and Hervé Varenne, *Americans Together: Structured Diversity in a Midwestern Town* (New York: Teachers College Press, 1977).

3. Sinha, "Religion in an Affluent Society," p. 190.

4. Ibid., p. 193; Varenne, *Americans Together,* pp. 55, 96-98, 127.

5. Sinha, "Religion in an Affluent Society," pp. 192-93.

6. Varenne, *Americans Together,* pp. 109-10.

7. This same insight is reflected in a study of the religious character of a church's life. The author concludes that the church did not help people understand transcendent experiences. See Jean Haldane, *Religious Pilgrimage* (Washington, D.C.: Alban Institute, 1975), p. 10. See also Andrew Greeley's report on the pervasiveness of "sacred" experiences in *Religion: A Secular Experience* (New York: Free Press, 1982), pp. 19-25.

8. This functional understanding of religion is seen particularly in the discussions of progressive religious educators. See analysis in chapter 4.

9. See, e.g., Huston Smith, *Beyond the Post-Modern Mind* (New York: Crossroad Publishing Co., 1982); David Martin, *The Breaking of the Image: A Sociology of Christian Theory and Practice* (New York: St. Martin's Press, 1979); E. F. Schumacher, *A Guide for the Perplexed* (New York: Harper & Row, 1977).

10. Peter Berger, et al., *Homeless Mind: Modernization and Consciousness* (New York: Random House, 1974).

11. See again James W. Botkin, Mahdi Elmandjra, and Mircea Malitza, *No Limits to Learning: Bridging the Human Gap* (Oxford: Pergamon Press, 1979), pp. 6-16.

12. We are indebted to our conversations with Richard Cookson of The United Methodist Board of Discipleship for this phrase.

13. Smith, *Beyond the Post-Modern Mind,* pp. 71-72.

14. Ibid., p. 134.

15. Sinha, "Religion in an Affluent Society," p. 194.

16. Smith, *Beyond the Post-Modern Mind,* p. 184.

17. Greeley, *Religion,* p. 23.

18. To name a few: Wilfred Cantwell Smith, *Towards a World Theology: Faith and the Comparative History of Religion* (Philadelphia: Westminster Press, 1981); Greeley, *Religion;* Charles E. Winquist, *Practical Hermeneutics: A Revised Agenda for Ministry* (Chico, Calif.: Scholars Press, 1980).

19. See Wilfred Cantwell Smith's brilliant discussion in *Towards a World Theology*, pp. 3-20, 180-94.
20. We are indebted to Michael A. Cowan for characterizing the U.S. condition and linking it to Max Weber's image. See "Sacramental Moments: Appreciative Awareness in the Iron Gate" (manuscript, St. John's University, April 7, 1983). The quotation is from *Max Weber: Essays in Sociology*, trans. H. Gerth and C. W. Mills (New York: Oxford University Press, 1958), p. 155.
21. Edward Robinson, "Professionalism and the Religious Imagination," *Religious Education* 77 (November-December 1982):631.
22. Michael J. Farrell, "The Resilient Father Andrew Greeley," *National Catholic Reporter* (April 30, 1982):9.
23. Andrew M. Greeley, *The Religious Imagination* (Chicago: Sadlier, 1981), p. 10.
24. Greeley, *Religious Imagination*, p. 17.
25. Greeley, *Religion*, p. 162.
26. Cf. Matthias Neuman, "Towards an Integrated Theory of Imagination," *International Philosophical Quarterly* 18 (September 1978):251-75. Here Neuman studies the status of imagination at the theoretical level and offers a construct for imagination that places it in a role equal and complementary to the cognitive in the development of the person: "The true fruitfulness of the human imagination comes when it leads to the process of authentic creativity whereby the person may reshape both self and environment to the mutual enriching of both" (p. 274).
27. Bruno Manno, "The Sacramental Imagination and Society: A Roman Catholic Contribution" (paper presented to Association of Professors and Researchers in Religious Education, Toronto, November 1979), p. 7.
28. Bruno Manno, "Ministry and Growth: A Reflection," *The Catechist* (forthcoming).
29. Martin Marty, *The Public Church: Mainline—Evangelical—Catholic* (New York: Crossroad Publishing Co., 1981), p. 3.
30. Virgilio Elizondo, *Galilean Journey: The Mexican-American Promise* (Maryknoll: Orbis Books, 1983), p. 167.
31. Herman Niebuhr, Jr., "Strengthening the Human Learning System," *Change* 14 (November-December 1982):16-21.
32. Charles E. Winquist, *The Communion of Possibility* (Chico, Calif.: New Horizons Press, 1975), p. 28.
33. Charles E. Winquist, *Homecoming: Interpretation, Transformation, and Individuation* (Missoula, Mont.: Scholars Press, 1978), p. 2.
34. Cf. James D. Smart, *The Strange Silence of the Bible in the Church: A Study in Hermeneutics* (Philadelphia: Westminster Press, 1970); Walter Brueggemann, *The Creative Word: Canon as a Model for Biblical Education* (Philadelphia: Fortress Press, 1982); James A. Sanders, *Torah and Canon* (Philadelphia: Fortress Press, 1972); Daniel Patte, *What Is Structural Exegesis?* (Philadelphia: Fortress Press, 1976).

35. David Tracy, *Blessed Rage for Order* (New York: Seabury Press, 1975), pp. 10, 11.
36. James D. Whitehead and Evelyn Eaton Whitehead, *Method in Ministry: Theological Reflection and Christian Ministry* (New York: Seabury Press, 1980), p. 177.
37. Ibid., p. 178.